BORZOI
BOOKS

FIFTY
YEARS

The Ignoble Savages

THE
IGNOBLE
SAVAGES

BY

Mariano Picón-Salas

TRANSLATED FROM THE SPANISH BY
HERBERT WEINSTOCK

New York • Alfred · A · Knopf

1965

L. C. catalog card number: 65–17385

THIS IS A BORZOI BOOK,
PUBLISHED BY ALFRED A. KNOPF, INC.

FIRST AMERICAN EDITION

Originally published in Spanish in Argentina as Los malos
salvajes *© 1962 Editorial Sudamericana Sociedad Anónima.*

... en lo más poblado están las fieras verdaderas.

(. . . the real wild beasts exist where the most
    men live.)

BALTASAR GRACIÁN

ACKNOWLEDGMENT

The translator wishes to thank Mrs. Walter Muir Whitehill for her numerous excellent criticisms of the translation, not all of which were accepted.

H.W.

Preface

The "ignoble savages" referred to in a chapter of this book are, naturally, a metaphor. It is a revealing one for an interpreter of culture, showing the extraordinary mental and moral disturbance into which a civilization has been precipitated which seems most anguished when we are supposing it most prosperous, showing, too, the break-up of its formative values without the emergence of others of comparable force and conviction. Between the world wars and the tyrannies accompanying them, the violence, conscription, and captivity suffered by a large portion of humanity took us back to the cruelest moments of the historic past. Multitudes yoked and

(**vii**

flogged like beasts have followed the combat vehicles of the Tamerlanes and Sennacheribs of the atomic age. Where had it gone, that universal citizenship of culture announced by Goethe and the prophets of the European Enlightenment? The poor victims—the intellectuals, workers, and bourgeois—whom the Nazis bore off to the gas chambers, must have asked if this was twentieth-century progress. The miasma of hatred, anxiety, and uncertainty could not be cleared from the historic horizon even after the final peace treaties. With its prosperous capitalism and its compulsively righteous socialism, the world seems, like the sleepers at Pompeii, to live on the eve of a catastrophe.

Before Friedrich Nietzsche died insane at the beginning of the century, he had announced the death of God, and perhaps his pride led him to believe that the God he wanted to destroy was going to be succeeded by the freest human sovereignty, the world of the "Superman," with greater clarity than piety and more energy than illusions. Prometheus would finally vanquish Zeus, captive man would be replaced by God in chains. What did that remote and "vaporous" divine kingdom represent as against the haughty kingdom of men? In the crisis that the epoch already had discerned, the Promethean task was to "turn the world around" so that "all values might be transalued." Although Nietzsche's prose rejected the vulgarity and optimism of the positivists (the fulfilled and abundant industrial society promised by Spencer), the new kingdom of the "Superman" might prove as closed and unbearably efficient as that of the Spencerian "technocrats." For man's greatness lies in his recognizing his own weakness, and the most dreadful of conceivable worlds would be one that had abolished all mystery, doubt, and secrecy, and had offered to all, blindly, its panacea of decreed and regimented happiness. The Leviathan State of our era always is eager to impose its authoritarian happiness upon us in the form of a police card or a vaccination certificate. In the name of that promise by the "third kingdoms"—fascism, communism, technocracy—how much blood, injustice, and opprobrium has been let loose upon the world. Even from the point of view of language, it seems the most inhuman of enterprises to exchange the Sermon on the Mount for *Mein Kampf* or the writings of Stalin.

Despite Nietzsche's inflamed prophecy, we do not know whether or not God died (how many people, captives and fugitives, were invoking Him along the roads of Europe between 1939 and 1945!). But we have begun to ask whether it is not men who have begun to die, whether they have not paid for their empty pretensions to being "Supermen." Either they burst open like poisoned rats in Hitler's subterranean den or they swung exposed to the wind and the crows like the corpse of Mussolini. The epoch that meant to supplant God had invented techniques for flying, production, and transportation, but it was not able to achieve human tranquillity. In our plethoric cities, men have done nothing for some decades now but give voice to a deep-seated anguish. Not satisfied with our own malaise, we acquire more anxiety in the theater, books, and the movies. The "spectacles" of Paris and New York are what was supplied to the hedonistic world of the *belle époque* by long-skirted cancan girls and the knees of *la belle Otero*.

Even literature and art, formerly the most beautiful and stimulating human adventures, the superlife, the super-reality that colored them, in the last decades have become too tedious; and after the inventions of a Joyce, a Kafka, a Picasso—great interpreters of the labyrinth and of all the metaphors and agitated dreams revolving in the consciousness of Western man—the arts of the West seem to have descended into an ice age of epigones. We have more formulas than creations, more theoreticians than creators. We go back to our Proust or our Balzac because we are bored to excess by Monsieur Robbe-Grillet. By a visit to the Louvre or the Orangerie we expiate a stroll through a strident Left Bank gallery where the wavering calligraphy of a drug addict is offered to us as the very latest art. The man of our epoch still does not know how to digest the immense civilization that he has swallowed; his stomach and mind have closed up; and he prefers to return to the panic and vacillation of the primitive. His autonomous rebellion now accepts no discipline, whether that of logic, drawing, and composition, or that of the daily bath. Some of the so-called "angry men" have taken on the desperate task of "decivilizing" themselves. No norm is necessary for incivility or "incivilization."

When culture is not denied, it can be masked with feints and simulation; a false new dress can be made from the plunder of an immense human legacy. As our museums preserve the booty of civilizations in fragments of things stirred together in any sort of emulsion—Javanese masks, totemic sculptures from Alaska, colors wrested from Claude Monet's great symphony, Mondrian's Calvinistic pentagrams, and the industrial detritus that can be rescued from garbage cans—we perform the teratological work of scandalizing the bourgeois, who, according to the best mythology, always must pay and be scandalized. Arts and forms of scorn, veneration of the coarse and the "paranoiac." The ignoble scholar vomits up his insomniac and pilfered artistic Encyclopedia, his *pot au feu* of floating forms in which a Mycenaean figure is joined to a Gothic gargoyle and New Guinean tattooing. A museum of man, but of a man upon whom the terrors of all the humanities that preceded him weigh, unreconciled. We are carrying the dead of all the earlier civilizations, disinterring them and devouring their bones because we lack the energy to create the clearly new. Our timorous era is looking for the world that must be born after the modern destruction of worlds, is looking for it with that terrible averted eye which seems to be seeking adjustment in more than one of Picasso's faces. It is the eye that searches for gods and fugitive men.

This is what in my book I call the "society of the ignoble savages," those who substitute traps, violence, and fury for the free-playing function of civilization of which Huizinga speaks. "A playing child is not puerile: he is that only when play bores him or when he does not know how to play," the Dutch humanist observed. And in the confusion of our epoch we have forgotten the rules of play, perhaps the controls and rites for mastering barbarism, and have declined rapidly into the most capricious puerility. In our lack of humor, in those conditioned reflexes which produce words and slogans charged with hatred, in the constant imputation of deceit and malevolence to those who do not belong to our sect, the great historian saw one of the gravest mental symptoms of our era, a renunciation of personality in favor of sinking back into the mass. Or the contrary: the autonomous trick, the delivery of their selves to dada and the absurd by those who want neither to build nor to be responsible. What prevailed after the crisis of democracy and liberalism was not man's sovereignty as promised by Nietzsche, but the fear felt by men who under the totalitarian dictatorships seemed to take refuge in a society of accomplices. New validity accrued to an old phrase of Baltasar Gracián's: ". . . the real wild beasts exist where the most men live."

In order to study these varieties of "ignoble savagery," an anthropologist no longer needs to go deep into the New Guinea forests or the wet Amazonian immensity. "Ignoble savages" write books, make revolutions, tyrannize over peoples, and appear in newspaper photographs every day. Others of smaller importance are to be met in some Paris cafés, well-groomed hermaphrodites and make-believe Robinson Crusoes inhabiting a forest of their own; they do not shave their beards and, as a result of imitating primitive men so closely, begin to act like them. In the ethical and esthetic chaos in which we have been living, there congregate in the same clouds of tobacco and marijuana smoke the Neanderthal man, the androgyne, and that impubic Lolita who was born perverse in a well-known scandalous novel. How easy it is to decivilize oneself, how much easier than to learn moderation, logic, and courtesy. Even the psychiatrists—so abundant and necessary in this difficult age—show us that if we but scratch a little the varnish of forms and styles with which culture has adorned us, we can hear our remotest pithecanthrope ancestor, confined to his irredeemable forest, howling in our subconscious.

But what I have proposed in this book is not a portrayal of customs—of the "ignoble customs" of civilized cities; nor, on the other hand, can I offer formulas of exorcism, contrition, and edification. I have no wish to be the kind of thaumaturge who drives demons from the soul as if they were worms. It may be that Lolita, the old libertine, and the *blouson noir* who sleeps with her and sometimes strangles her have existed in all epochs. The Bluebeard of French legend did not have an apartment in Saint-Germain-des-Prés or the vicious Place Clichy, frequented by activists, drug addicts, and homosexuals. Nor shall I begin shouting at the world because a few "angry" young men have stopped going to the barber shop, have taken up arms against the Louvre, and have sworn enmity against the "Mona Lisa." The theme of my reflections was man's destination and how he best uses the culture that he bears on his shoulders, which seems to inundate rather than impregnate him. And I wanted to see if, after so much frustration and anguish of the sort that our contemporaries live through, we could get back to that state of conscious evolution under man's direction, that continuous and progressive "anthropogenesis" of which Father Teilhard de Chardin spoke. Perhaps like that great French Jesuit, a witness and wanderer in the lugubrious hours of Europe's worst night, the victims of the Nazis—those who were about to perish in the gas chambers—looked up at the sky for the last time to ask if the universe makes any sense. Perhaps, that is, we are addressing ourselves to what he called a distant "point Omega," to the hope of another constellation.

Paris, April 1962

CONTENTS

The Ignoble Savages

Berlin: Twenty Years Later

❧ · SOCIOLOGY OF THE APOCALYPTIC

Twenty years after the Second World War, Berlin still is the skeleton city of Europe, the immense burned and empty shell, recalling one of the greatest dramas of Western civilization. I speak of the two Berlins—West and East—because man's tragedy transcends all ideologies, and neither so-called Western capitalism nor Eastern communism has an exclusive formula for peace and human tranquillity. Naturally, the observer will say that the Berlin of the Federal Republic was repaired and remade more rapidly than that of Pankow, but on both sides of the Brandenburg Gate a frontier of ruined buildings, a

(3

common rubble of horror, and empty stretches of earth mark the sites where pompous Wilhelmine or Hitlerian structures once stood. It can be asserted that West Berlin abounds in shops, hotels, and splendid cafés that are lacking in East Berlin, that the street life on the terraces of the Kurfürstendamm during one of those summer twilights crowded with businessmen and tourists offers tremendous animation in contrast to the long tedium, to the few faces and the rare automobiles crossing the Stalinallee at the same hour. But beyond these economic facts (West Berlin belongs to a zone three times richer than that of East Berlin; millions of United States dollars flowed in to reconstruct German industry after the devastating war; the prosperous markets of the entire Occident were opened to the drive of the Federal Republic), I should like to penetrate, on one frontier as on the other, into the testimony and drama of the spirit. I have no wish to serve any propaganda by saying that on one side of the Brandenburg Gate everyone is happy, on the other side of it everyone miserable. I do not believe in that absolute goodness which, depending upon the speaker's ideology, is said to be exclusive either with the Marshall Plan or with the so-called "Soviet liberation." For the moment, it sufficed me to know that on both frontiers all the people were Germans and were deceived or self-deceived, all were involved, all were suffering in the same manner. One of the paradoxes of the great divided city is that the monument to the Russian soldiers remains on the west side, whereas the Hohenzollern palace stood on the east until it was demolished. But today Berlin is not only a neuralgic ganglion of the contemporary conflict, something like a perilous gaming table, but also a microcosm of the Occidental anguish of the last thirty years. It was the scene of a Wagnerian drama in which those who perished had thought themselves gods. Among the vestiges left by the destruction I even found a certain Kantstrasse, the street of the philosopher Kant, as if that name had in itself been a promise of moral redemption.

How many witnesses of the tragedy we meet in the streets of Berlin or mark by their preoccupied presence in the subway train in which we go from one zone to the other at the hour of heaviest traffic. I observe to Germán Arciniegas, my excellent and most avid traveling companion, that all of the people in our car except a girl of thirteen or fourteen must have witnessed the catastrophe. They bear something like a scar of their anguish on their perplexed faces, in their taciturn gravity. Many of these people are reading the afternoon papers, and we realize that they must read the evening's news with more cautious and agitated preoccupation than people in any other city in the world.

No modern European nation had received as many gifts of God, balanced by temptations of the Devil, as ever-youthful, turbulent, hard-working Germany. The myth of Faust, of somehow being re-born, always was its myth. And in the complicated process of rebirth, Germany—like Faust—emerged from its laboratory, from meditation among its books, to search for the most nocturnal adventure. It could have redeemed itself through science, but at times felt the need to frequent the Walpurgis of the witches. It had captured in systems the most per-fectly decanted reasoning of the Occident, only to end up by negating it and sinking into irrational chaos. It arrived late in modern history, when the colonialist and imperialist powers had divided among themselves the seas of the world and its dis-tant continents, and therefore projected, in explosive interior adventure of "torment and impulse," the ocean that it lacked, attempting thus to satisfy its appetite for expansion and for space. But that Ger-manic *Sturm und Drang*, which Goethe, Kant, or Schiller, like orchestral directors conducting a tem-pest, wanted to subject to norms, was to turn into a terrible autonomous force when it changed into the will to dominate, when Germany wanted to make the other peoples of Europe pay for the circumstance that it had appeared late at the table of partitions, influences, and imperialist power. The land of poets, musicians, and philosophers thus contradictorily became the land of the *Junkers* and of total war. The other face of the Goethean "universalism," of that ecumenical citizenship of culture about which the great poet-minister once spoke, could develop into choleric nationalism, into the mystical infection of the "elect race." Did not the Prussian state, with its parade of force and its bellicose hierarchy, frustrate the humanizing impulse that could have brought it the democratic influence of liberal Europe and the inspiration of its philosophers and poets? From the time of Frederick the Great on, the kings of Prussia read illuministic tracts on peace and tolerance—so as to impose war. The "Empire" was reborn at a time when everywhere else emperors, with their title and its dangerous medieval association, had begun to disappear. Already Heine had made fun of that attempt to resuscitate and re-uniform the Teutonic Knights in a century of industry and liberalism. The German economy moved forward toward the most modern forms of production while the state was yearning to adorn itself with the armor of medieval warriors. During the nineteenth century, from 1848 on, and more acutely after 1870, this dichotomy produced a conflict between the German state and German culture. That conflict, which already had provoked the sarcasm of Heine, may have contributed to giving birth to precisely the Marxian apocalypse, the poetry or the sociology of the exiled.

Have we realized sufficiently how much romantic reaction against his own position in life, what strange affinity with Heine's sarcasm, lay in Karl Marx's first insights? The youthful intellectual exile who, in his Parisian lair during the tumultuous winter of 1848, wanted to formulate a new philosophy of history and establish the determinism of revolutions, behaved like one of the prophets of Israel announcing a new kingdom of God the Avenger. A few streets from Marx's garret, M. Comte was awaiting the more peaceful and reasoned evolution of human communities which would accompany the development of an industrial society in which science would direct politics, the metaphysical stage of history give way to the positivist stage. But Marx preferred to summon us to that earthly Jehoshaphat whence the bourgeoisie would go to eternal flames, the proletariat ascend to a classless Paradise. Was not his announced proletarian state—the dictatorship that was to be the final consummation of history—like the other face, the vindicating face set against the state of the Prussian *Junkers*? Perhaps that poetic and prophetic flame, the fire circulating below the logical reasoning, was what gave Marx the strength that he would not have achieved with only a theory of history and political economics. Against liberal evolutionism he set up his tragic idea of an apocalypse.

Nineteenth-century German life developed as a reaction against or an apology for the Prussian state. At times such philosophers as Hegel and historians like Treitschke seemed the heralds or apologists of Bismarck. In the universities science must be put into hierarchies as rigorous as those established for the army in the war colleges of the Empire. The Bismarckian *Kulturkampf* no longer resembled Goethe's universalism: it was intended to be an instrument of domination and to replace the spontaneous voice of the people. Bismarck had no fear of socialism—a word already uttered often in his epoch—if he could impose it as a decree of the Iron Chancellor and not alter the hierarchical structures of the German state, and if the workers would express their gratitude for it in the most disciplined march-past. And did not that hypertrophy of the hierarchical overisolate German science in its erudite fastnesses and render it impenetrable to ordinary intercourse? How much of Brahmin caste there was in that strange society of dominating *Junkers,* professors emeriti, military men, great managers, an anomalous society in which history books and encyclopedias seemed allies of Krupp cannons.

In the catharsis of his madness, Nietzsche also wanted to bring about the dissolution of those false values of force, of too much pomp and too much smoke, which in his epoch already were blinding the German intelligence or diverting it from its universal destiny. Zarathustra went up into the high mountains so that men should see and understand better. And to destroy Philistine conformity and servitude the "Superman" must arrive, the dauntless dancer and cruel alchemist who would transmute everything. In Nietzsche, as in Marx, the evils of the time engendered a consciousness of apocalypse, and the catastrophe was lying in wait beyond all those overvalued or merely apparent goods. A most profitable study could be made—like one of those diagnoses of the recent past—of the forms of the apocalyptic in German thought from Marx through Nietzsche to Spengler. To the revolutionary mass that would destroy the bourgeoisie and impose the classless society, Nietzsche opposed an inversion of all the problems of conscience, as if man were to return to that moment of solitary perplexity and terror in which he had not only to define the world but also to assert his being in the face of things; and he all but recommended—in the homeland of so many historians—a

therapeutics of "anti-history." Spengler, on the other
hand, announced a stormy wintertime for the history
of the West, cataloguing the symptoms present in
our culture which had signaled the congealing and
death of other cultures, such as that of the Roman
world. Perhaps in our century—as in Rome from the
third century on—we would pass from the Caesarism
that replaces the moral and legal order in crisis to
the revolt of the marginal classes and peoples. First
the state—as in Rome from the time of Diocletian—
would be transformed into a monstrous machine of
oppression; then the slaves would welcome with
pleasure the arrival of the barbarians. Possibly when
Spengler wrote his final pages on the eve of Nazism,
a sort of epilogue to his monumental work, he could
only think that the totalitarianism of Hitler and
Stalin would exceed that of Diocletian, but that after
them—to return to his parallel—the colonial peoples
would launch themselves against Europe. Spengler,
too, had a *Junker* mind, and the future apocalyptic
movement was to be that of the "colored races"
against his old Aryan and blond friends.

❦ · AND BERLIN IS THERE

And Berlin is there on its drained Brandenburg
swamp, surrounded by lakes and woods, as if awak-

ening from a nightmare that burned out its eyes. From the Friedrichs and Wilhelms through the time of Bismarck and ending with that of Hitler, it was built as the capital of force, and it was transformed into a capital of flame and ashes during the most horrible nights in European history. Seventy-five million cubic meters of rubble accumulated in 1945 on the wide avenues of former times. From the Brandenburg Gate, through which, in the imperial dream, the most warlike soldiers of Europe had marched, friezes and columns were borne away. The freezing multitudes made firewood and charcoal from the well-cared-for trees of Unter den Linden. The subway was flooded, and the bodies of the final victims of the shipwreck floated in black water impregnated with soot, dust, and sulphur. Another inferno of horror had been turned upon the "non-Aryans" in the gas chambers. In that final hour the dominators and the dominated both paid. Dr. Rosenberg, the *Führer*'s pseudo-philosopher, had not foreseen whither his demonic myth of the twentieth century was heading. Cultivated German reason had lived for twelve years in exile, silence, and captivity.

Some of the greatest dangers of our civilization were exemplified in a shuddersome manner by the Nazi tyranny. It was the moment at which Frankenstein's monster assassinated his inventors, at which propaganda maneuvered by a group of loudmouthed men tried to drive out the memory of many centuries of teaching contained in many books by the greatest thinkers and moralists of the Occident. Even the tranquil parishioner who went to his Lutheran church each Sunday and sang psalms became a follower of armed demagogues preaching that the blame for everything had to be worked off onto the Jews and agreeing with Rosenberg that creating myths and believing in them was preferable to clarifying truths. A son could denounce his father; the Gestapo worked to end all temptation to think. Nazism was the most tragic flight from and renunciation of the European moral consciousness.

In the balance of history it is not necessary to impute all the guilt solely to those groups of resentful and frustrated men who began to follow Hitler, who destroyed synagogues and beat up intellectuals and Jews, who organized the "nights of knives," the alliance of homosexuals and assassins; for judgment also should be passed on the other Europe that did not isolate the catastrophe in time and was even incapable of denouncing the crimes to the "League of Nations." Were European morality and humanism divisible, isolated, and confinable? Could the France of Blum and the England of the first Labour governments reconcile themselves to the Germany of

Hitler? Instead of penning the wolf in time, the great nations wanted to make arrangements with him and pacify him with new rations of innocent blood. Will we oppose Hitler because of the thousands of Jews made to suffer in the concentration camps and die in the gas chambers or because of a few slave provinces that the *Führer* wants to incorporate into his empire? And for the rout at Munich, Mr. Chamberlain appeared with an umbrella, as if with it and his phlegm he could divert the hurricane that was battering Europe.

After the apocalypse of the others had been produced, the bombs that fell on Berlin between 1943 and 1945 seemed the expiation of Nazism. In the last act, on the long road of death which ran from Stalingrad to Sicily, passing through the ashes of Rotterdam and the ports of Normandy, there was left of Berlin—the ultimate goal of the Russian, English, and United States divisions—only an immense furnace beside which a lunatic in a striped shirt gesticulated. The witches, his astrologers and fortunetellers, had promised him dominion over the world. He sank his highly cultivated Germany into an immense prelogical night of auguries, conjurings, and pacts with the Devil. But that delirious man and his fury also were buried in the remains. Over Berlin had to fall the cruelest winter that the history of Europe had

known since it was invaded by Attila, since Asiatic
hordes came to pasture their horses on the Danubian
plains.

Now Germany has risen again, and the Siemens
buildings and the Hansa quarter of West Berlin look
too much like a city in the United States, just as the
rigid buildings of the Stalinallee in the East sector
are not unworthy of its name and recall Stalingrad.
Faced with the travel bureaus and their colored
posters and offers of summer trips to Italy and the
fjords of Norway, the Mediterranean, or the mid-
night sun, or sitting on the cosmopolitan terrace of
the Hilton Hotel, where prosperous and spendthrift
people dance the cha-cha, one could believe that the
horror and the terror now are remote. And are not
this capacity for resurgence and forgetting, this return to making and to adventure, this leaving behind of the night of nightmare and rubble, native to
human nature? Need not each generation forget the
perplexities and anguish through which its fathers
lived? Some of the youth of the world—the part that
is not very rebellious, existentialist, or Robinson-
Crusoesque—dances to the same music everywhere,
combs its hair in the same style, and reads the trivi-
ally perverse books of Mlle Sagan. Others, more religious, perhaps pray to the Saint Hedwig of the
rebuilt Berlin Catholic Cathedral or to that Saint

Barbara whose expeditions and martyrdoms were so often painted by the German primitives of the Middle Ages, asking that no Third World War occur.

Again there are wooded walks in the Tiergarten, and children and nurses, and mirrors of water; again the well-fed, well-trained animals of the Zoological Garden fulfill their public function of entertaining the passersby. The Berliners always took pride in their Zoo, as in their museums, as if these places brought them that geographical dream of distant climates and landscapes which sleeps in their studious, adventurous soul. With the nomadism of a habitué of overnight inns, Hitler and his bands never considered what they could offer to Europe of the peace and meditation of the great German spirits. He saw them as false warriors of Arminius, not as builders of a civilization. Without realizing it, he wanted to transfer Europe's problems back to a world of disintegrated races and frontiers in which he could be the New Charlemagne. His vengeance complex never let him understand that the Germanic already had debouched into the European.

And has not modern civilization learned to look at and classify everything that gives form, heat, and color to the earth: the organic and the inorganic, the plants, lava, algae, and crystals that petrified the geological ages—learned how to do so because in the best hour of European science there were always

German eyes, German lenses and hammers to probe
and to classify morphology and species? Humboldt
and Ratzel were geniuses as characteristically German as Goethe, Bach, and Beethoven. And the world
still has need for that investigatory tenacity, for the
German book, microscope, and hammer that have
penetrated all the strata.

While I was visiting Berlin, a colloquium on the
philosophy and ethics of liberty was being held in
the Kongresshall of the Western sector by educators
and humanists from the widest variety of latitudes.
What could Europe still offer, not only to its own
peoples but also to the many new nations wanting
to rise from ignorance and colonialism to the highest
levels, to full political determination and responsibility? Humanism or oppression—is not the dilemma
more tragic now than in that nervous dawn of
modern history, that century of geographical and
moral discoveries when a few thinkers began to set
up—in opposition to abuse by princes, intolerance
by the churches, and hatreds among states—a new
sovereignty of reason and an idea of justice that
could be established above parliaments and privileged classes? I saw among the Hindus, Africans, and
Europeans attending the colloquium the ascetic,
nervous face of Robert Oppenheimer, who was smok-
ing his interminable pipe. Who better than one of
the great investigators of nuclear physics could tell

Europe and the present generations of the magnitude of the challenge of the times and the resulting responsibility? For saving, maintaining, and increasing the goods of culture and human equanimity and tranquillity, a courage exists which is colder and more necessary than the physical courage and aggression in which a large part of man's contradictory historical adventure has been consumed. Is not this the lesson best deduced from the landscape of Berlin? The feeling of guilt that surges up after contemplation of these ruins of the Second World War, the monstrous warning of what another war could be, plants the seeds of a saving compromise beyond what is called capitalism and what is called communism. Now it is not a question, as in the diplomatic history of earlier times, of defending "European equilibrium," the "balance of power," or the geographic-dynastic frontiers of the churches or ideologies ("*cujus regio ejus religio*"), but of the whole future of our unfortunate species. Even in the splendor and wealth of present-day Europe an apocalyptic uneasiness persists.

❦ · GUILT AND RESPONSIBILITY

During recent years, a large part of the West's thought and literature has dealt insistently with its

18)

guilt complex. Sartre's play *The Condemned of Altona* is a confession of horrors for which no absolution remains possible. But the protagonist who, from his haughty, cruel position as an ex-official of the Nazis, degenerates into fear, neurosis, and defeat, into complete contempt for men, into likening himself to the ugliest and humblest zoological species, finds no way of appeasing his anguish except by begetting new crimes. It could be said that "We are all criminals!" is the single idea floating upon the protagonist's confusion and living destruction. Well, then, we are as repugnant as the crabs and deserve to be crushed. To demonstrate that belief and shut off all hope of redemption, this modern Oedipus too—gloomier and of much smaller stature—will commit incest and parricide. Must we not extirpate the whole race of crabs? Some men weep like hysterical females and assassinate like executioners. Torture is a form of amorous unfulfillment. And have we not, in our epoch, seen sinister dictators torture their peoples and commit mass assassinations because, according to their ideology, they loved humanity too much and possessed the absolute and inflexible formula for human happiness? People have been murdered even as a pretext for increasing production, accelerating industry, and issuing daily bulletins of more optimistic statistics. Numbers have been valued higher than men. Fortunately—and this is the power of Christ as against the Antichrist—the Sermon on the Mount speaks not of numbers, but of souls and suffering people.

Those who saw Sartre's play in Paris that winter and paid for their orchestra seats and drank champagne during the intermissions commented—as is the habit—on the theatrical technique, on the ability of the actors, and on whether or not the philosopher of *Being and Nothingness* had had recourse at times to the most stridently melodramatic devices. That story, then, did not seem to the Europeans of 1960 as remote as the legend of the Atridae? But the question is much more complex than the style or the technique of the work and the elements of tension or interest which it awakens in the audience. Sartre has been one of the most persistent denouncers of the guilt of our culture, and during that moment of confusion and of prescribing for a new epoch which some French intellectuals were living through after the Second World War, he began to wonder if the afflictions and dislocations of the West might not find a way out through the world of justice established in the East. Was the dove of peace which the communists had adopted as their emblem, like that which Noah sent forth after the Flood, going to descry dry land and hills bursting into flower? "Corrupt capitalism and pure communism . . . old society and new society . . . world of blame and world of innocence" —did not those antitheses seem too Manichaean for a spirit as intelligent as that of M. Sartre? But the account given out by Khrushchev after the death of Stalin perhaps finally convinced the most compromised intellectuals that the idealized world of the East was not as just and as innocent as propaganda had been picturing it; Beria and some of the terrible purgers of the GPU, for example, would have fitted into the hair-raising world of *The Condemned of Altona*. What engendered the present conflict in history was not merely a collision of economic systems —capitalism and communism did not correspond strictly to Marx's visions and prophecies—but a deeper, anthropological confusion. Had man been deprived of that "unity of meaning" with which he had been endowed by the old morality and rights? By subordinating the idea of justice to changing and accidental facts like "the revolution" or the needs of a single class, had we destroyed the essence and universality of the idea? Hitler said that whatever served the National Socialist state was good and just; Stalin seemed to reply that the good was what permitted the carrying out of his five-year plans even though thousands of people might perish and innocent men proclaim their guilt. From that condition of the modern soul in which the state and the myths of power associated with it had greater force than any church ever had had in history, that moral inferno had developed, the price of the guilt in which the "condemned of Altona" had their being.

Sartre's existentialism admirably described the solitude and "nausea" in which man was struggling. The entire literary *œuvre* of the French writer offers a labyrinthine sampler of the European soul in the hour of its greatest anguish. Sartre's apocalypse does not even lead to a changed future, for it seems to be participated in by man himself: the inferno is born inside his consciousness. But after the confession and conflict of guilt, which are the predominating theme of Sartre's dramaturgy, one is entitled to ask what new road can be opened to the Western spirit. I do not doubt that the method of purging man of so many illusions and conventions, of ransoming him from the things that weigh upon him so as to confront him with himself and place him in what Jaspers would call the "extreme situation," has been conducive to a more realistic view of history. The drama of the "condemned of Altona" is that of people who lose their myths only to subsist with their crimes. That neither "German honor" nor the "war against our enemies" justified treason and transgression would be the simple Christian lesson to be learned from the play if Sartre accepted Christ's morality. But without questioning himself or answering himself much—the theater is not a philosophic treatise— he prefers to unleash the tragedy and thus familiarize people with horror. The Europe of today is not as securely optimistic as that of Queen Victoria and Bismarck. Sartre doubted the "white man's" mission and superiority, the imperialist myth of Houston Stewart Chamberlain or Cecil Rhodes, the myth in whose name Hitler burst forth. He therefore began to perform his existential psychoanalysis.

A formula of cure or sublimation must be sought for the guilt complex acknowledged by European civilization; it would be acknowledged also by the communist countries if their press and literature were not under rigid censorship by the state and if that state did not order its writers to be happy. Psychoanalysis would limit itself to pornography or to the chronicling of *faits divers* if it merely stuck to a description of the case and did not aspire to being a radical therapy. The cure does not lie in the guilty person's doing away with his accomplices and finally committing suicide, as in *The Condemned of Altona*. The only cure is that of accepting an ethic of responsibility, a thing perhaps more difficult than the expiatory elimination that is a frequent resource of Sartre's dramaturgy. Has existentialism flourished as the description of a disease without being able, even yet, to found a morality? Or does it romantically invoke the "true revolution to come," as if it must carry away in its avalanche the remains and products of a perverse species? At times M. Sartre, like a new archangel with trumpet, offers himself as a guide to that rendezvous at an atheist Jehoshaphat. Or perhaps he is preparing to send down from his apartment in Saint-Germain-des-Prés a revised Mosaic decalogue, having noticed that the Ten Commandments appear to have become insufficient for the fury of our times.

Berlin, crossroads of two worlds, the place in which the catharsis of an evil moment in European history was being achieved, made me reflect upon this problem of the contemporary conscience. Will the world of the two frontiers—Oriental and Occidental—have need of a new synthesis of what it should believe and hope, just as, in another time of anguish and dogmatic polemic, the theologians at Nicaea had to reconcile themselves by drawing up the Christian Creed? In the ethical and juridical confusion of our time we must go back to learning what is right, what is just, what is criminal. For some totalitarian states forget these matters too quickly, and a false morality of success and power has legitimatized the most atrocious crimes. The new and inescapable problem is one of human recuperation and responsibility, a problem more important than the conflicts between a capitalism that no longer is so much that and a communism that does not resemble Marx's Utopia. Perhaps our epoch has tired of counting horrors and following the trials of its hangmen, and is seeking values that can reintegrate it, can re-establish the "unity of meaning" for the man who is not solely a communist or a capitalist, a proletarian or a bourgeois, but a person pursued by questions still asked in the name of a universal law of justice. *The Condemned of Altona* painted the tragedy of a generation and an epoch, but we have the duty to demand of a person as intelligent as M. Sartre that he succeed in teaching us—finally!—how our guilt complex can be sublimated in responsibility. In Germany, as everywhere despite those who preach salvation exclusively through economics and statistics —we must not only rebuild the factories and demand that the Siemens structures be stronger than those of 1938. We must also reconstitute the spirits of men.

Visit to the Ignoble Savages

❦ · WHEN THE MARQUISES WERE NOT

TRANSFORMED INTO SHEPHERDS

The dream of the Golden Age: the projection
onto an already senile and lost age, or onto an oncoming age, the hope that man will behave himself
better and that the lights of reason or the cleansing
of sensibility will make him more tolerant, more
benevolent! The last great polemic about the perfect-
ibility or imperfectibility of humanity was carried on
in European literature after Rousseau wrote his dis-
courses on *Whether the Re-establishment of the
Sciences and the Arts Contributes to Improving Cus-*

toms and on *The Origins and Bases of Lack of Equality among Men,* and when an older and infinitely more foxy Voltaire replied to them in his admirable letter of August 30, 1755. Attuning its reasoning and summing up and clarifying in it all of human experience, as the best articles in the *Encyclopédie* set out to do, or, on the contrary, adopting that candor and spontaneity before the world which Rousseau recommended, the aging, weary European civilization of the eighteenth century could dedicate itself to the enterprise of producing better men. The virtuous and the sensitive prevailed over the violent and the tyrannical. Voltaire, who had studied English institutions, who had advised Frederick the Great and wanted to teach Pompadour herself "to be reasonable," thought that perhaps those in power should know as much history and have as much capacity for analysis and discovery of errors as the author of *Le Siècle de Louis XIV.* For Rousseau, on the other hand, the operation was simplified down to the recovery—in the face of the malice and perversion of the times—of past, lost innocence. For Voltaire, it may be, the best men would be those who succeeded in being as cultivated, perspicacious, and elderly as himself (in some ways he was the Nestor of a libertine Europe), whereas Rousseau wanted to transform the overdressed and perfumed marquises and abbés of the rococo epoch into eclogue shepherds. Or on some exotic island peopled by "noble savages," virtue, fidelity, and veracity unknown to the courtiers of Louis XV would reign. For the one believed that the remedy for humanity would be a constant increase of culture; to the other, it seemed better to jettison and forget the excessive ballast of forms, conventions, and prejudices which European civilization had accumulated. But what the "reasonable" and the "virtuous," the fanatics of "illumination" and of "natural goodness" did in the days of Thermidor became too well known, and the establishment of happiness by decree of the public authority remained problematic. Locke had said cautiously that imposition of improvement by decree usually engenders tyranny. Nor did the problem of human improvement change in any radical ethical sense when, against the redeeming "noble savage" of our anthropological disease, Marx opposed the equally innocent "noble proletarian" as the instrument that would redeem us from the abuses and injustices of the bourgeoisie.

The problem of employing the savage state as an antidote to the ills of civilization—as some physicians treat certain nervous ailments with a dose of the barbarians' curare—has changed much since Rousseau wrote his two well-known treatises; and some anthropologists of modern life who, instead of continuing to study the inhabitants of New Guinea, have investigated the customs of Hollywood or of some "existentialist" *caves* in Paris have reported forms of primitivism that would scandalize the author of the *Confessions*. Savagery used, not to recover the Adamic or Edenic innocence that we lost, but to deliver us over to the absurd and to make the norms of life infrahuman is demonstrated in some recent theatrical pieces, such as those of Beckett and Genet. The proposal now is not that of metamorphosing the marquises into shepherds in search of innocent spontaneity, but of descending into savagery by denying almost the entire moral legacy of history. (Whereas Rousseau believed that savages perhaps were free and happy because they only had to adapt themselves to the contingencies of their natural world, later ethnography was going to destroy the entire illusion of "noble savagery" by discovering that, on the contrary, savages lived captive in a confused and terrifying animist world and that magic and the concept of manna provide no cure for our excess of historic consciousness.) With almost greater abandon, some characters in the contemporary novel and theater live out their lives while swimming in that chaos which Lévy-Bruhl's old terminology would have labeled "pre-logical." To reduce man to the biological limits of the amoeba was the total purpose of this conversion to the irrational in which, as a reflection of this age of anxiety and nausea, recent literature has involved itself. The somber protagonists of Beckett, from inside of their garbage cans, moving like larvae among the filthy refuse in the great intemperateness of their hopelessness, scarcely succeed in stuttering into life. In this case, the "return to natural and spontaneous primitivism" proved to be not a conquest of confidence but an abandonment to fear.

The argument between Rousseau and Voltaire seemed to have been won by the Genevan when the history that followed them contained more irrational factors than reasonable ones. Chapters of that battle in the life of the last two centuries were: Romanticism, disheveling heads and disordering hearts; psychoanalysis and all the psychologies of the unconscious, exploring the dark platform on which the libido was hiding; and, above all, certain sorts of torture and "concentrationist" politics which the highly civilized twentieth century was to experience. Thus, just as the palafittes of some primitive peoples were built on the mud, it was enough for the piles upon which the complex structure of our society was erected to be shaken a little for us to detect the stench and slime of the subterranean mud. To stop

being civilized was easier than Rousseau had
thought, and the examples of barbarism stopped
coming from the *"tristes tropiques"* described by
Lévi-Strauss. Especially between the third and fifth
decades of the present century, between the March
on Rome of the Fascist blackshirts and the end of the
Second World War, men lived in an epoch of "ignoble savages." The marquises were not transformed
into shepherds, but at times nobles, bourgeois, and
proletarians knew how to change themselves into
executioners. Is it certain—oh confused Rousseau!
—that literature and the arts have contributed to the
corruption of manners and the moral decadence of
the human species? Between 1940 and 1944 the fast-
est trains carried to the gas chambers a fearful, incessant cortege of prisoners. At the death camp they
were awaited by the new executioners, transmogri-
fied into professors of chemistry. An epoch so proud
of its technocratic exactness had to make inventories
of their skin and bones, the grams of metal set into
their teeth, and the small amount of grease that their
bloodless bodies still could be made to yield up.
Adolph Eichmann was the scrupulous functionary of
the German Third Reich, a faithful servant of the
other one, the great Adolph, and he never erred in
his statistics. Jews were transported to death as one
might transport Ruhr coal, potatoes, and beets from

Pomerania, or wheat reaped in the fields of France. During those years, all of enlightened Europe, with the spires of its churches, the gilt of its baroque palaces, its libraries, porcelains, and tapestries was agonizing. Far from Rousseau's dream, what was set up against the imperfections of our civilized world was not the candor and spontaneity of "noble savagery," but savage cruelty and cannibalism. Europe was peevishly devouring its own culture. We had doffed the waistcoat and vest that had oppressed hearts uselessly, not to rediscover natural spontaneity, but so that all the hatreds of *Pithecanthropus* could palpitate.

❦ · THE CHURCH WITHOUT RITES

"Believe in the irrational, in blood, and in the race" now that it is impossible to believe in the transcendental—that was the cry of the beerhall demagogues who became converted into Nazi executioners. Or do not believe in anything, live the adventure of total emptiness, gladden yourselves with the ruin of all the values of a world that has neither meaning nor way out, and in which everything is uncertain and contingent—such is the anti-dogma of contemporary nihilism. Such were the rebellion of autonomous violence and that other rebellion of nothingness, the great theme of the last novels of tsarist Russia, between 1905 and 1914, the epoch of Andreyev and Artsybashev. And the weariness of culture, the lack of confidence in culture, did not succeed in preventing atrocious wars, but produced, back there in 1918, the babblings of dada. Let us form syllables, spontaneous onomatopoeias like those of a child discovering its first sounds. On the ruins, by spontaneous generation out of the putrefaction, a new culture will be born—so those "angry men" at the end of the First World War thought. Contemporary history began to resemble a church without rites into which the profaners' horses and vehicles of war had entered, and the tribe was castigated by its gods. It was a society of aggressively lonely individuals, in which neither the sign nor the ceremony created the unity of the group, and every archetype lost its validity. At times people united sporadically, like the most primitive clan, in a foray of extermination against the clan beyond the frontier. The new fury of the ideologies—those false religions of the desperate—taught the proletariat to hate the bourgeoisie, the bourgeois to silence the voice of the proletarians. The bombs of terrorism answered those machine guns of the illegitimate powers which were mounted on the myths of hatred and of class domination. And sometimes—as had begun to happen in

Russia under the tsars—the terrorists were on the payroll of the police. The traitor was formed from the repentant fanatic and vice versa. A frenetic humanity, inflamed against every moral norm, bursting the uniting image of the group, had to create the concentration camp. We had denied the inferno of the other life, the final term given to the guilty themselves, but only to anticipate it in immediate sadism. The pen of Herr Eichmann went on writing in his Gothic calligraphy the number of those sacrificed each week. How confined the themes of the great novels of the nineteenth century seem, even suffering as understood by Dostoevski, when faced with this pain of entire peoples and races, with this human herd bleating in the slaughterhouse of the Gestapo!

And it turned out that all civilization ceased to be civilization when its unifying rites and norms were eclipsed by autonomous discord and fury. Thus, aggressive and fearsome solitude became the persistent theme of contemporary literature. In Sartre's *No Exit*, that the group be confined in a hermetic space without possibility of escape suffices for its members to be suffocated by incommunicable helplessness. Their greatest punishment is that of finding themselves together, and it may be that they would welcome joyfully the arrival of an executioner with an ancient demon's brand to scorch their flesh, to liquefy the grease of their guilt. But they have to be where they are, trapped as in an immense insomniac night, under an unchanging light, each separated from the others by his own specter. What is lacking to re-establish dialogue is language and human affection, what Christ called charity. The heterogeneous sum total of their frozen solitudes is incommunicable. Or, as in the famous painting by the Norwegian Munch, the astonished faces—the woman with the headdress, the rigid men in the high-crowned hats—are waiting anxiously for something terrible to happen, for the world to end, or, worse, for their waiting to be prolonged into infinity. Lacking the capacity to give himself or to be integrated with others (this is perhaps the symbolism of Munch's painting), man now waits alone for an external catastrophe, a gratuitous cataclysm that will determine his destiny. Let nature or death, Eichmann's final gas-emitting douche, decide what his own free will cannot even consider. Munch's figures stand one beside the other, one crowned hat next to another crowned hat, one woman next to another woman, but no one is looking at anyone else's face because every gesture that might bring them together has disappeared from among them. They share no song or rite, no dance or speech.

In that summary of gratuitously malign péripeties we were catechizing ourselves as to how the epoch had gone wrong. What had happened to the canons of beauty, conduct, and courtesy in which our fathers' generation still could believe? "Civilizations are mortal," Paul Valéry said often enough. And as against the dream of progress and "perfectible humanity" of the European Enlightenment, we men of this epoch felt during the Second World War, and have not stopped feeling even now, the threat of a collapse of the entire Christian culture. What would the world have been if the Nazis had triumphed? Or perhaps hope is to be found in the humanity of the technified ant heap, of insects using tractors, as promised by the Chinese communes? For, like the good Père Lebret sending his disciples to the Congo or to Guinea from his school in Paris, we ask how to realize that synthesis between economics and humanism, between technique and creative liberty, in which the discord of the ideologies can be ended.

To civilize the ignoble savages into which we civilized people have been converted is an enterprise for a new Émile, who, like Rousseau's protagonist, has dreamed of, and then become disenchanted with, the revolutions that change things without improving souls, without giving our aggressive solitude either hope or companionship. Rousseau wanted to

inject into the Europe of his time, which already had
begun to show wrinkles, the restoring hormone of
noble savagery. Stripping themselves of their pe-
rukes and star-decorated jackets, the marquises were
going to transform themselves into shepherds and listen to forgotten nature. The Queen of France—the
one whose head later was cut off—would assist at the
milking eclogue of her Versaillesque and highly civilized cows. Goethe remedied both his juvenile temptation to commit suicide and the troubles of the
young Werther by means of a double invitation to
the serene harmony of the classical forms and to
primordial astonishment when confronting nature in
forests and cascades. The verses of the *Odyssey,* the
marbles that seem verses and the verses that seem
marbles, and the light of the Mediterranean whence
Nausicaä emerged were reviving to the poet during
his travels in the South. Later, time became more
anguished. The man of our epoch no longer knows
what to choose so as continue living in a Babel world
poisoned by the planetary spoils of many civilizations.
He has become the crazed proprietor of an inheritance that cripples him. He sees and touches testi-
monials of man's adventuring through many centuries, but because he has so much, he now does not
know whether to prefer the Greek or the Hottentot,
the Hellenic statue or the tribal mask. In fact, in

certain mongrel creations of present-day art the Hellenic is ground up in an emulsion with the Hottentot. Expression of the frightful is preferred to discredited beauty. And so ethnographers who had dedicated too many books to the Papuans and the afflicted inhabitants of the Marquesas Islands began to discover that we too, in the worst hours of our century, still suffered from fear in the face of primeval chaos. We were in danger of transforming ourselves into an irredeemable species: that of savages who once had been civilized. No cannibalism exceeds the crimes committed by Nazi Germany when witch doctors and executioners took over the function of interpreting destiny.

❧ · NAUSEA AND COMPANY

At the end of the 1930s, perhaps from 1935 on, when all the Nazi bonfires had been lighted in Germany and the vast Soviet excommunications had begun, existentialism was perhaps the most widespread philosophy of the West, its most immediate reaction to the horror. On the one hand, the totalitarian tyrannies had reduced man to an "implement of the party," an automaton who obeyed catchwords and clothed himself in the myth so as not to have to think for himself; on the other hand, psychology and literature were being complaisant about that human fragility which results when the structure of consciousness is erected on the slippery mud of our "complexes" and our libido. We were moving about the world as though on a cracked, narrow platform below which the subterranean magma, the lava from the volcano, boiled or the cracks of tectonic faults showed. Or we were like a certain sort of savages, improvident walkers on piles that seemed to dance in the dirty water. To begin in weakness and helplessness; to accept the radical recognition of error offered us by reason and by the crisis of the values that were being profaned, maltreated, or destroyed by the imprudent men who had taken charge of history would have been better than to accept the false "good conscience" of impresarios of the collective lie. A terrible moment of catharsis and fever began for Europe. In the second part of *Faust* the four old women—Mangel or instability; Schuld, or guilt; Sorge, or anxiety; and Not, or human misery, followed by Tod, death, which devours all—surround the palace and unloose unstanchable discord. They had been metamorphosed, with greater power than in the time of Goethe or that of Kierkegaard, into the Parcae of our civilization. And the Sartrean personage, engulfed in a monstrous world in which forces and powers had swollen beyond man's dimension, could feel only "nausea" in the face of what was all around him. That "nausea" was the proof of life and of consciousness, just as thought was their proof under the great rationalist and Cartesian illusion. I live, I exist, because I feel nausea—that was the sole mark of our individuation in the chaos of nature. Starting from our nausea, we began to order or disorder our piece of the terrified universe.

Beyond the peripety of the Sartrean personage, no God rewards or punishes, no transcendent goal makes life more tolerable. We are in the embrace of our own guilt, agitated by our own nausea, which alone is truly our own and personal, the pestilential lamp lighting our absurd circuit. And because outside ourselves—beyond the "in me" or "for me" in which man recognizes himself—no values and archetypes exist, or because man's own adventure and compromise alone can establish them, life becomes fragmented into discrete situations. And at times we, the "ignoble savages," ask ourselves if, like real savages, we are going to react with primitive astonishment and panic to each event and each thing. How can I discover solidarity or charity in this anomalous congeries of untransferable, incommunicable solitudes, seeing that my nausea is not your nausea and that only I can experience the peril to which my existence subjects me? To foresee only persecution or shipwreck—as happened to us during the war—is what Sartre's dramatic characters achieve, sometimes with a pathetic strength that does not disdain the resources of melodrama. Or in those moments of deeper reflection, in that play of "reversing the world" which Hegel thought the most passionate adventure of philosophy, the idea of God becomes mixed with the idea of the Devil, the boundaries between the good and the bad become imperceptible, and the traitor is identified with the liberator, as in more than one scene of *Le Diable et le bon Dieu.* The fact that Sartre has illuminated the moral labyrinth and helplessness of our epoch, that he shows man the modicum of refusal of which he can avail himself against the depersonalizing pressure of the great contemporary myths, and that he has exposed "nausea" as a new fount of knowledge and a species of solitary civil war between "being and nothingness" —these achievements do not signify that Sartre has opened new roads of conduct to us. How shaky and full of pitfalls his "roads to liberty"! They offer no firm footing upon the insecure quagmire of our times. For want of an ethic, he presents us, as few others present us, with an impassioned description of the Western spirit in its hour of greatest anxiety, in the most convulsed hours that Europe has lived through since the Reformation.

And how they weary us—because they miss all finality—those mixtures of autonomous adventure and experience of the new Robinson Crusoe solaced in his own shipwreck which some recent books and confessions proffer. Mlle Beauvoir, Sartre's companion, talks to us, in her profuse volume *La Force de l'âge*, about the character of life, its avatars and preoccupations, between the eve of the Second World War and its unleashing. But when from isolated "nausea" of discontent with the world she rises toward no teleological goal, life appears to be fragmented into a sheaf of episodes, a description of isolated phenomena. We follow Mlle Beauvoir in the animated, at times fatiguing and variable, description of her juvenile years. *"La force de l'âge"*—*"la fuerza de la sangre,"* as Cervantes said better—is not a sufficient justification or explanation of life. Having emerged from the university with one of the most agile female brains in France, Mlle Beauvoir wants people and things to instruct her just as books offered her a university degree. And that "course of improvement" will be the cafés of Paris, with their parade of eccentric characters, the chance friendship of people who wander about with their rebellion, their disorder, and their originality, that variegated anthropological fauna made up contradictorily of homosexuals, rebels, and candidates for frustrated genius. One eats and sleeps badly, talks to excess, changes friends and lovers, experiences everything without absorbing anything; existence dissolves into saraband and frenzy. Mlle Beauvoir, whose vitality never tires in this book, loves and perhaps venerates M. Sartre, but can it please her to be present and note the signs of other loves and experiences in which their mutual restlessness is discharged? Are not both of them too intelligent and perspicacious to subject all human beings to their disillusioned analysis? The private is confused with the public until it almost appears monstrous in this book, in which a bad dinner, an erotic episode, deviation, and some personage's secret are written down with unvarying cruelty. Beyond the life of a rebel against bourgeois order who fled from home with the ill will of a prodigal son and did not succeed in achieving other saving values, events as agonizing as the Spanish Civil War from 1936 to 1939 were happening. But even the terrible Spanish war seems to become merely a subject for talk, for will-less frenzy, as it is lost in the labyrinth of personal adventures, in the coming and going of overexcited people. Does not the passion for justice which Mlle Beauvoir stirs up become a little lost, during her twisting itinerary, in *ballets russes,* 1936 films, the rhythm of jazz in the nocturnal *caves?* For to talk about the Spanish war and comment on it

(43

from a Paris café does not mean that we are assuming our ethical responsibility toward it. An intellectual's "clear conscience" also may be false, a way of absolving by words what he has not had the will to seal by acts.

To what point is life only the exchange of excitations and sensations, the simple adventure of a prodigal son escaped from home and now asking for new surprises each day without knowing where he is going or what is the reason for his travels? This is what we ask while reading Mlle Beauvoir's book. The question to be asked of this fable is: Are so many comings and goings, so many turns and returns, of some use? And, as against certain existentialist explosions and expressions, it can be asserted that the problem is not so much to live as *how* to live. And perhaps for that reason the author's most human and believable pages are not those in which she wishes to reveal herself to us as very acutely modern and intelligent, but other, simpler pages in which a woman called Simone (she might have been called Jane or Mary) goes—during the war—to visit a soldier named Jean-Paul Sartre at the garrison where he is serving. Many French women were going to visit husbands, sons, and lovers in the war zones; they were enduring the cold and privations of difficult trips; they were sleeping in bad village hotels; the anxiety of the writer was not different then from the anxiety of the working women as they waited together for the door to the ward to be opened and for the orderlies to take pity on them. In that dialogue of a man and a woman in danger there is no literature, paradox, or ingenuity; suffering and need dissolve all rhetoric; the intelligent are on a level with the slow-witted, and a common destiny humanizes and levels into the same anguish the disparities of life.

And the fact is that to live is more than to collect sensations or to make an inventory of the despicable. To say that we are guilty and that the world has disgusted us does not suffice for shaping a morality; we must rediscover the norm of civilized man out there beyond the sadistic experiment, beyond life as a continuous explosion and spectacle. Present-day literature and philosophy demonstrate excessively how we have stopped being civilized. *La Force de l'âge*, Mlle Beauvoir's biographical testament, does not seem to me very edifying. Any young woman who had passed through the Sorbonne and Left Bank cafés with the same curiosity would have been able to say the same things. To destroy the "bigotry" or "hypocrisy of culture" to which Sartre once alluded does not signify that we can confront life with impunity or that, as in the drama *Le Diable et le bon*

(45

Dieu, each one of us may exercise autonomously the office of priest, warrior, or prostitute. Europe seemed to have forgotten the hope for a perfectible future which the *illuminés* were seeking. The "noble savages" invoked by Rousseau had lost their qualifying adjective. During so rich an epoch of ethnographic science we were learning that civilization might ape the terror and the mask of primitive man. During the war totalitarian tyranny and terrorism took us back to the chaos of forces outside our reason and our will. The four horrible hags of the Goethean myth were haunting the palace. "Where is hope?" we asked after reading all those biographies of prodigal sons, the testimonies of fury, disdain, and solitude which the epoch had accumulated. And life itself, Mlle Beauvoir's *"force de l'âge"* is not precisely the force of conscience.

News of the Devil and of France

🌸 · DIABOLIC FOLIAGE

The affair with the Devil began this way: for a long time I wanted to write a study of the excessively inventive and joyful demons whose exuberant foliage of masks, attitudes, and vices penetrated even the tympana and columns of French cathedrals, and whose gesticulations and perpetual "horror" contrast with the hieratic attitudes of the saints and the blessed. All the free imagination not permitted by sacred iconography was displayed by Romanesque and Gothic sculptors in their representation of these devils, to whom they assigned extra faces in the stomach, faces confused with the bellows blown or

(47

the caldron boiled, and to whom, in the most unexpected places, they gave the sexual forms of serpents
or toads. Sometimes the rural demon of the medieval
sculptures seems to be a toper and a glutton who
has drunk all the Burgundy and eaten the rich-
est cake, who pinches women or tries to trap angels
at the very solemn moment when they are weighing
souls. All this seems to be the ghost of the good or
bad digestion of an epoch in which the winters and
the nights were felt to be longer; at the castle they
cooked the heaviest meat of the wild boar, and even
the erotic ideal of the epoch looked upon woman
(despite the chivalresque idealization) as another
hunted piece to be devoured with more appetite
than cunning. Simply prolong the species in whatever way. People died young, and forty years meant
old age—and from time to time the horrible plague
passed through village and castle with its reaper's
scythe and the rattle of its spiked collar. Rout out the
witches who may have poisoned the wells; or exor-
cize the demons. When the image of the Devil was
not a nightmare or some explanation of gratuitous
and inexplicable evil, it was, on the contrary, a flight
of repressed fantasy, the violent, vital expression of a
world that preferred to the personal and the concrete
the abstraction of "universals." Thus the portraits of
the Devil made by medieval sculptors (oh, much-

admired Gislebertus of the Cathedral of Autun!)
sometimes are only a caricature of an entertaining
copain, of a happy friend with whom one has shared
wine, rich mouthfuls, laughter, and the companionship of girls.

A friend of mine who is a cultural historian said to
me that in France the Devil himself (if we except
terrible stories like that of Bluebeard) was not meant
to produce greater ravages. And we should recall
that in each hour of great peril, God has granted
France a valiant and very wise saint or virgin as
shield and buckler of its people. To liberate so enchanting a city as Paris from the barbarians, He inspired the activity of Sainte Geneviève; against the
English, and to the end of reunifying France, He
armed Jeanne d'Arc. Against the violence of the
Prussians in 1870, He erected a wall of piety and a
new pact of the Virgin with the French land, the
miracle achieved by Bernadette. And even against
the frock-coated anticlerical ministers of the early
twentieth century—such as those who made up the
Combes cabinet—He opposed the edifying story of
Thérèse of Lisieux. Only after the Second World
War, according to my historian friend, no virgin appeared, and the reason was that an antithesis to vir-
ginity was set up, the slightly demoniacal myth of
Brigitte Bardot. But to what degree is Brigitte her-

self really demoniacal? Is this demon given flesh by her writers, directors, and publicity agents? That was the prior question that I was trying to answer before passing on to more serious matters.

❦ · THE TEMPTATION OF BRIGITTE

During a recent autumn, discussion arose as to what amount of the diabolic could be found in the Brigitte case. "She was found unconscious at the edge of a well in the garden," the newspaper stories said. In the background of that landscape—what an irony!—as if in invitation to eternal pleasure, the Mediterranean rippled most diaphanously, a luxury yacht waited, and the perfect landscape was completed by the red hills and the marbles, cypresses, and oleanders of the Côte d'Azur. A landscape for the rebirth of Venus.

But was Ophelia's conflict going to repeat itself in existentialist France, which seemed to feel no compunctions about love and sin? How small the resemblance to Ophelia of this physically promising girl whose erotic splendor not only ignited the enthusiasm of the crowds, but also hung over French finance and was more worthy of being immortalized on banknotes, had more legitimate right to that honor, than Victor Hugo or Cardinal Richelieu! How could a girl who at the age of twenty-six had more than one million francs for each of her years, and to whom life could offer neither obstacle nor boundary, suddenly experience the same downfall as the humble daughter of the old courtier at Elsinore? Ophelia was nothing but a sweet servant admitted into a powerful society of evil individuals, whereas, on the other hand, Brigitte inaugurated an empire of eroticism in which neither social classes nor frontiers mattered. The one, to please her infirm prince, would adorn herself with field flowers, whereas the other preferred those mineral branches which the jewelers of the Faubourg Saint-Honoré provide to millionaires eager to give presents. One invites us to the melancholy understanding of solitary love, the other to the universal insurgence of modern pan-sexuality. Ophelia would weep over the turncoat condition of her lover, whereas many men will suffer because of Brigitte. But when anguish seizes them, they behave alike. Or can it be that these dramas of the self against itself cannot be explained by the formulas of historical materialism and by the differences between a courtier's daughter and a millionaire "star"?

Perhaps it also can be asserted that the evil of Brigitte did not result from her own dereliction, but was the product of persecution, publicity, and evil desires on the part of her many admirers. The convinced Marxist would say that in the more innocent communist countries the same thing could not occur. The fact is that when, after some hours, the confused queen of the world awoke in a clinic and asked only for the repose of a pillow, much darkness, and silence, she said: "I can't stand it any more." And in silence and darkness—while the Paris dailies launched extras telling us the degrees of her temperature, the words of her delirium, and the rate of her pulse—she would meditate on the hateful, almost painful fame that her managers attributed to her. Did she, in fact, represent present-day amoralism, the unchained power of sex without sanction, religion, or obligation, or was she simply a good, ordinary girl to whom had been attributed perversely sins that others did not dare to confess? "Am I to blame for having been born too beautiful?" Brigitte could have asked those who sat in judgment on her. Too, her attempt at suicide could have been charged to the account of the theorists and cinematographers of the so-called *nouvelle vague,* who could conceive of nothing happening between a man and a woman but the incessant, pitiless civil war of the sexes, pleasure as annihilation. It is a more sadistic myth than that of the Amazons, that of Achilles and Penthesilea in Kleist's drama. Desire becomes independent, almost separates itself from the loving person, and instead of becoming integrated in happiness, is realized in fragments as homicide. The smoke, the drugs, and the insomnia of the huge modern city provide it with a background crueler than the field onto which Penthesilea sallied in search of Achilles while all the verdure of spring burst forth.

And it may be that the real drama of Brigitte is that of a girl who, though she seemed able to do anything, could not do what was within the power of any French girl of her age and station: go to an amusement park with her badly dressed sweetheart, take a ride on the Ferris wheel, rush over the scenic railway, and afterwards share the refreshment and ham sandwich of poor couples. But when she appeared one night to have a peaceful *café crème* with one of her directors in Saint-Germain-des Prés, reporters and photographers spied on her at once in order to launch a new witticism. Is she getting a divorce or isn't she? Will she find a new husband? Has she fallen in love during the past twenty-four hours? A perverse drama is attributed to her whenever she agrees to be seen in the company of a male friend; likewise, no man can draw near without foreseeing slaps and scratches. Now she cannot listen in peace, in a thoughtless group of young people, like thousands of French girls—and without the most irregular designs being attributed to her—to the blues

(53

and the spirituals, the syncopated outcries, reeking of rum cocktails, in the existentialist bars. Because advertising teaches that everyone should desire her and confides to her the dangerous mission of being a plenipotentiary of sin, all pursue her with teeth-gnashing fury. Whom Brigitte will love is no longer a problem of her own and of the man she pleases, but of the huge mouths of gossips who never stop gnaw-ing at her life. (In our technified epoch, the old folk-loric role of the gossips is exercised by the evening press.) This new sort of Ophelia, who wanted to go to sleep at the edge of a well, was being pursued by all of Macbeth's witches and their crow-like cackling.

The Devil, if he exists, has carried out against poor Brigitte an exploit very different from that of the medieval demons. He is not the same Devil, he of the seven well-known, well-defined capital sins, the old choleric Devil, gluttonous and lewd. An inventor of more abstract relations and intrigues, this Devil not only delights in the commission of the transgres-sions enumerated in the most venerable theology, but also forges new sins, sins against the spirit which could not be foreseen when Moses wrote the Tablets of the Law and the doctors at Nicaea summed up the fundamental precepts of Christian ethics. How inno-cent and primary those devils—masked, libidinous, and drunken—on the old French cathedrals! Are not these other offenses of intelligence's cold-blooded invention, this rancorous cult of evil, so deeply rooted in contemporary man worse than the gluttony of meat and wine? To have no peace or tranquillity, to attempt to prove our real existence by mortifying others and ourselves—these are the commandments of the new decalogue. We seek nausea, which for Sartre is the proof of existence, as the mystics of another time sought ecstasy as a way of approaching nearer to God. In the story of a good girl—such as Brigitte Bardot perhaps wants to be—an expression of the demoniac prevents her from leading a normal life as an elegant young bourgeoise who has prospered. She does not want to allow herself the spontaneous and untransferable enjoyment of seeing herself in the mirror, contemplating her jewels, driving her automobiles, having a good time with a friend, or feeding her *caniche,* as thousands of women can who are neither diabolical nor aspirants to the palms of sainthood. *La Verité,* a Bardot film shown in the French movie theaters—the theatrical tension of which doubtless had some influence upon her crisis of the preceding year—*The Truth* made it clear that a tragedy would occur wherever she appeared. (Whereas the cinematographers of the United States, more ingenuous than the French, surely would have taken advantage of Brigitte's amorous

(55

exuberance to make her into a beautiful new Mae West whose films would have had happy endings, the *nouvelle vague* directors cannot bear a gram of happiness and delight in attributing disasters to her.) Crushed by her perverted renown, the poor girl wanted only to weep and disappear into limbo. Whereas other young girls in equal trouble were going to confess to a priest, she chose to do it with barbiturate tablets.

🌿 · THE TRUFFLE IN THE ASHES

One of the most refined dishes of the French cuisine is the *truffe sous les cendres*. It seems that *haute cuisine*—like refined eroticism—prefers to the product offered by nature that which the chemistry of time has transformed, bleached, made bland. Primitive man preferred that the animal he had succeeded in hunting should be eaten while its blood was still fresh and its meat still warm. Civilized man persists, on the contrary, in keeping meat until he has made it completely tender by cooking it. God made the useful things in nature, from woman's body to the tomato, the carrot, and the truffle; the Devil preferred to invent sauces. And when we people from other, less civilized places, eat our first *truffe sous les cendres* in France, we have the impression that we are being offered a strange disinterred product. It may be very attractive to an educated palate, but when I taste it in a Paris restaurant, I cannot dissociate it from a terrible image of paleness and disinterment. Are not ashes precisely, in the commonest symbology, the sign of destruction and of mortal gelidity? The *truffe sous les cendres* seems to be a food of those chthonic subterranean gods, those gods of dampness and the sepulcher, whom the Greeks knew before the warm clarity of Zeus burst forth. The modern Devil whom we want to interrogate seems much like the *truffe sous les cendres*.

I usually see him—with the pallor of a night-living creature (the Devil does not sleep), with his long hair disarranged (for now the hairdressers are paid to *dis*arrange hair *à la mode*)—surrounded part of the time by those young girls whom the language of the epoch calls "nymphettes" (they have ceased to be virgins without having succeeded in becoming women) and taking his nocturnal Pernod in the taverns of Saint-Germain-des-Prés. (In defense and description of France, I want to say that these cafés and taverns, even though they were frequented by M. Sartre when he was the young author of *Les Mouches,* have nothing to do with the limpid, systematic French culture. But they give to many frustrated people, to tourists in search of extravagance and to little boys and girls who have fled their homes, the illusion that they are very intelligent and are taking part existentially in the drama of the epoch.) From the *blouson noir* who attacks the humble gasoline-pump attendant or who, with the same gasoline, burns a cabaret girl in the Forest of Fontainebleau, to the bearded youths of Saint-Germain-des-Prés, an inflamed rebellion of young people who do not know how to adjust themselves sanely and normally to the world is something like a sign of the times. The carpenter's son no longer is content—as his predecessor was in other centuries—to be a carpenter; equally, the son of a bourgeois is not satisfied to work in the bank that gave security and prosperity to his father. Be he a student of philosophy, he dreams of running the risks of a now non-existent *maquis* or of dedicating himself to the most nocturnal terrorism. Those young people are awaiting a new Balzac to interpret their turbulence. Like the so-called "Monsieur Bill" of a recent crime, they are potential parricides who, when unable to eliminate their parents, try to cover them with infamy. They go out happily and without preoccupation to take walks with their grandmothers after having murdered their lovers—or are they begging their grandmothers for the human tenderness that their lovers could not give them? The peculiar morality of what in France is called the *milieu*—which at times infects certain intellectual groups with cruelty and nihilism —forces them to be hard, reduces to the bitterest calculation of self-interest and egoism anything that they undertake, so that many of the "nymphettes" who follow them also resolve to be "hard." For in the full equality of the sexes no experience that a man can undergo—however dirty and disagreeable it may seem—is considered inaccessible to a woman. Disillusioned with yesterday's values, they do not succeed, in the confused moral shipwreck, in seating themselves at a table of other values. And in the meantime they must live through Paris's excitations in the form of new erotic invention and a continuous peripety of the absurd. Their heads become swollen and blackened with evil thoughts, like a truffle underground. *"Je t'aime, je t'aime!"* Monsieur Bill screamed hysterically at the mistress whom he had not succeeded in strangling, and because he was so faithful to her, he wanted to marry her there in the jail. Of course—for the world cannot be so completely sorry a place—there are innumerable other young people who rise early to complete their university degrees or work in a library, factory, or laboratory. Because of them, the population increases. They have good habits, take care of everything in its time, write books, make scientific discoveries. They

(59

are the people relinquished by the Devil's hand—for
the world has become so demoniac that this must be
pointed out, just as, in earlier days they spoke blas-
phemously of those who had been "relinquished by
the hand of God."

❧ · IMAGE OF THE INFERNO

The Devil, whom in my metaphor I have called
Monsieur Truffe-Sous-les Cendres, is to be found
fraternizing with the members of a group or reading
France Soir to find out "if reality is greater than fiction," in any of the—to me—hideous cafés of the
Left Bank. Insomniacs turn so pallid that not only
does the nickname I have given him fit him, but his
veins appear to contain the very liquid that is in the
glasses of Pernod. No trace of that red and sumptu-
ously masked Devil of the medieval sculptures! This
one seems anemic and too angular. He also has lost
the emphasis, that free gesticulation and agility of
hand with which he played such pretty tricks on
angels at the moment of the sorting-out of souls. But,
as if proving the laws of evolution, what he has lost
by way of talons and dancing dexterity, he has
gained in discursive precision. Nor is he interested in
peopling his Inferno with vulgar reprobates—glut-
tons, drunkards, aged misers, and fornicators—such

as he used to put in the old pots to cook: he is interested in the society of subtler people. As part of the specialization imposed by the times, in order to enter the Inferno one needs a doctorate or its cultural equivalent. And the Devil himself could be taken for a technician or wise international expert. He is a passenger on all the jet planes, always is returning from a secret mission to one of the countries in which a conflict is taking place. And he can talk in an unchangingly monotonous, coldly documented voice about astronautics, politics, and abstract painting and literature. He takes advantage of the most scrupulous bibliography without revealing it much. Of such a personage, so dehumanized and sure of himself, who has replaced emotions with data and sentiment with rigorous calculations of probability, anything can be expected: that he will organize a cold act of terror against the prime minister of a distant republic or inspire an adolescent's suicide.

"What is the Inferno like now?" I asked him that night when, perhaps convinced that because I am old and already have been tempted too much to become dazzled by new temptations, we were talking about evil and diabolic matters with the objective calm with which we might have talked about a revolution in Laos.

With a lecturer's pauses, he began to answer.

"The Inferno," he told me, "is nothing but one final destination of men, what in earthly language might be called the crowning ornament of a profession. Thus, just as many wise men aspire in old age to be members of the Académie or to earn the Légion d'honneur, so others do everything required to gain entrance into the Inferno. But just as men have evolved since Gislebertus carved the drama of blame and sin in Autun Cathedral and made such fun of me, so that final habitat has changed in accord with the needs and, I might say, the tastes of the wicked. The medieval Inferno closely resembled a crude castle kitchen: bad ventilation, an excess of soot, dirty pots, and souls being singed like hunted animals on the charcoal. A decoration—too romantic for the modern sensibility—of legendary serpents and dragons. A continuous fight of gladiators to which they drove me by means of the armed Saint Michael, and which seemed to reproduce—for the Inferno also is inspired by earthly life—the struggle of the great vassals with the king of France. Today nobody would believe in such an Inferno, and if it still exists, it has been preserved merely as a historical monument to make good 'spectacles de son et lumière' during the tourist season.

"It could be shown to spectators like those cold, ferocious castles of Louis XI, not yet illuminated by

the light of the Renaissance, in whose dungeons
bishops and nobles fallen from royal grace were left
to rot. A diabolic, intriguing, evil-smelling king, not
fit even for the Inferno itself. But for other men, another crowning torture—as though the mere fact of
living were not that already, as some existentialists
affirm—one more consonant, too, with the progress
of architecture and of human customs. We had a
Renaissance Inferno with classic motives, Roman
columns, and a decoration of gilded arches which the
Borgia family loved. We had a baroque Inferno and
a rococo Inferno that Pompadour wanted. In the
pedantic words of our epoch you could say that we
have evolved in accord with the historic situation
and that now we have a functional Inferno that can
be displayed decorously at architectural expositions."

"What is it like?" I asked my erudite companion.

But the Devil (who is that for this reason) answered me with another question: "Have you ever
read Kafka's novels or lost your way on a dark afternoon in the cellars of the UNESCO Building here in
this very city of Paris? The new Inferno can be compared to both things, which apparently are oppo-
sites, but really reveal the very soul of the epoch. It
is like the new Chancellery that Adolf Hitler
dreamed of and more or less like the one in which
Comrade Stalin smoked his pipe while seated in an

armchair. There you would see, bespattered with the ashes of their victims, some of the Dachau assassins and many pale people indoctrinated with the cruelest ideologies of our twentieth century. Less lustful and gluttonous than in the Middle Ages (how innocent the sins of the flesh appear today, when even the Marquis de Sade cannot frighten anyone!), but abounding in sinners against the spirit. You know that illiterates go to Limbo, which may be the only advantage of the so-called 'underdeveloped countries.' But, as you also know, the Inferno is reserved for men of great human lucidity such as Herr Rosenberg, Hitler's private philosopher; Herr von Ribbentrop, his chancellor; and Herr Himmler, his chief of police. There they have the opportunity to do what politicians who lose power always do: carry out exercises in self-criticism."

"I understand all that, but why did you include Kafka's books and the cellars of UNESCO in one image of the Inferno? They are cultural works, peaceful works furthermore, and I cannot imagine why they should be alluded to in an inventory of infernal realities," I said, interrupting my interlocutor.

"That metaphor was merely a provisional explanation, which is a common quality of all metaphors. Kafka brought to modern literature the image of the labyrinth, that of a man lost he knows not where, pursued he knows not why, a symbol of the fact that we are burdened down by sins that we do not recall having committed. A Kafka protagonist can go to bed a man and innocent, only to wake up changed into a lawbreaker, an orangutan, or a worm. And it is as if he were in the cellars of the UNESCO Building that the protagonist of that terrible novel *The Trial* moves forward down a very, very long corridor—a corridor about which he does not know whether it leads to an exit door or to an electric chair—where there are many identical offices and, as on the higher floors, many papers. And when it seems that we have reached the end of the corridor, an arrow directs us to the beginning of another, which leads to still another, until the giddy brain does not know where it is. What difference could it make to the protagonist of *The Trial* that a corridor is numbered 1, 2, or 3, when through every doorway he sees the same functionaries sorting out or writing the same documents? Creating, as in Kafka, the trial of 'the trial'—doesn't this strike you as a marvel of technical organization? And why employ medieval caldrons and embers and legendary flame-spewing dragons when we have worked out a colder, more systematic cruelty? A cruelty that leaves no footprints behind and, instead of reddening or charring its victims, turns them pallid and gives them the look of thinkers.

"Nor does the judgment of souls require that set

of scales which in the Romanesque and Gothic imagery we disputed with the Archangel Michael, and on which adulterous women, old lechers, and simoniac priests came to be weighed like animals. We amused ourselves in those merry days by mixing up on the same side of the balance the tiaras of popes, the crowns of kings, the nooses of the hanged, the canes of lepers. Nowadays that is too much, for the differences among men are not decided by office or estate, but by conscience, and each being is preparing his own trial as long as he lives. In our era, many people are born in the Inferno and stay in its climate without ever becoming acquainted with more stimulating landscapes. Therefore, they think themselves powerful and liberated, like my good medieval damned, who, when I threw them into a caldron, thought that I would have to respect their former human condition as princes, gentlemen, bandits, or concubines de luxe. 'Everything is lard in the frying pan of the Inferno,' I used to say to my acolytes. Even I have lost the sane humor of those times and am beginning to resemble my victims. Haven't you noticed that this Saint-Germain-des-Prés atmosphere is not very healthful, and that sleeplessness, electric light, and the sometimes very intelligent discussions tend to turn us too pale?" the Devil asked in conclusion.

❦ · MEDITATION WHILE NURSING A PERNOD

The Pernod, drunk iced and colorless, resembling the Devil's tongue and certain misty Paris winter nights poorly furnished with stars, was becoming exhausted in the glasses. Would we pay for a new round to the health of the Devil? For that Saint-Germain-des-Prés café, with the faces of its anemic frequenters, victims of their insomnias, and the clientele of old libertines, incipient *blousons noirs,* and "nymphettes," might be compared to the anteroom of the Inferno. How little gaiety and candor in its conversation! How horrible it is to seem to know everything and never to feel admiration or surprise like a child or a peasant! What, then, were we going to beg from the Devil? All of us were satiated to overflowing with the rottenest fruits of evil; they were in the soul, more than in the body or the sex, of the men. Nor does the relationship with sin now consist, as with the very human sinners of the Middle Ages, in eating just once a whole boar's rib or emptying all the winebags or pinching all the girls or ending all quarrels with bloodshed. Like the characters of Kafka, the modern condemned man goes on wandering in the labyrinth or loses his spirit in a series of Chinese boxes and cannot recover it. Everything is aseptic and well ordered, but he cannot free himself

(67

from entanglements. Like one of Kafka's protagonists, he may embark for America. But he may never
reach America, or the America that he is seeking
may be fragmented into an interminable series of in-
cidental Americas. He will never rejoin his friends
and family; he will lose all love for his fellow crea-
tures and drop the thread of his first projects. One
day when he awoke from a nightmare and looked at
himself in the mirror, he no longer knew whether he
was man, worm, or orangutan (since a monkey has
traveled toward the stars, all the species have become
mixed up). Nor, as in the Middle Ages, can he escape to the Holy Land to redeem relics from the
infidels or go in search, while overcoming monsters,
of the rose of perfection or the goblet of the Holy
Grail. If bourgeois society disgusts him, he will be
able to join a clandestine or illegal party, but there
they will set him to writing papers and repeating
slogans (which are repeated and repeated without
being analyzed)—for should he dare to speak a
spontaneous word, he can look forward to a trial
more secret and shadowy than that of Kafka's character. We were born into a humorless world that has
little use for laughter and jesting.

Like a new Saint John the Divine isolated with
his horrible dreams, a young, neurotic Prague Jew
described and prognosticated that dead-end struggle

which involves today's souls. Now every adventure has been tried; every revolution engenders counter-revolution; so-called culture does not conquer cruelty, and at the gate to the temple, forsaken man vainly invokes gods who have fled. Splendid cities arise; every day towers higher than Babel's are raised or a group of sages uses extremely precise calculations and experiments to kill more than two hundred thousand people. More than were exterminated by being impaled or tied to war chariots during the long reigns of Assurbanipal, Nebuchadnezzar, and Sennacherib, kings not far from wild animals.

And the inexpiable drama, the real infernal secret, is the disintegration of the entire system of forms and values which once established man's relative security. The modern Devil is an engineer of disintegration. More than the atom has been disintegrated—for the plutonium of all the rebellious souls also has been fragmented and is ready to explode. Who can say now what is really beautiful or really right? The problem of values no longer is clarified during one of those Platonic colloquies seeking perfection in some approximation of our anguishing sensual world to the pattern of an intelligible universe. Nor, beyond men's passions, are there, as there used to be, ideas or archetypes with which to define equanimity and beauty so that—as among the

(69

Greeks—the philosopher's advice lay close to the sculptor's canons. For in the newest diabolic sport, the word or concept that I use has a different meaning as used by my antagonist. Each group or sect has its own peculiar dictionary. Just as the capital sins used to exist, and medieval theologians used to range them in numerical series, each sin corresponding to a very special circle of the Inferno, so now transgressions arise from the distinct significances that we give to words and things. Man's universal morality has been exchanged for the ethic of the partisan and the fanatic. For lack of that "sweet fruit" of which Dante spoke, we find the feeling of transcendence assigned to action, work, and life. Existence is as unfortunate an activity as that journey to America which the Kafka character undertook, for the spirit ends up by losing all sense of project and volition.

Sex no longer must be sublimated in love, and we make of a French girl the protagonist, perhaps the martyr, of autonomous sexuality. When she faints like an unseasonable Ophelia, we will revive her because "experience"—more important than feeling—interests us all. And "The Truth," what the director calls "the truth," is the sum of the cruel experiments not disguised by piety or tenderness. Whereas in other epochs—such as that of Romanticism—commiseration and tears were abused, today they are

exchanged for unpardonable transgressions and in-
fractions. So as not to return to the sentimentality of
his grandmother's stories and the pruderies of a
bourgeois household, "Monsieur Bill" resolved to
make himself "hard" and to murder and incinerate
one of his mistresses.

"Men are like that," he said when he reached the
taverns in the Place Clichy. What a great satisfaction: to be certified as "hard" and to be the principal
subject of several editions of *France Soir*!

Many men transfer "disintegration" and "hard-
ness" to other forms of action, such as politics, and in
the name of my own idea I have the right to eliminate those who doubt or do not accept my Utopian
state or society. If I am a revolutionary, I shall eliminate my enemies as counterrevolutionaries. If I am a
defender of the status quo, I shall shoot them so as to
forestall the "revolution." What would be unpardonable would be for me to leave life and speech to
those who do not believe in my formulas, which are
completely adequate for imposing human happiness.
Today sociologists and economists exist to say that
the suffering and hunger of one or several generations do not matter if the plans that the Devil's ex-
celling engineering has prepared can only be carried
out in the future. The slogans say that they will
suffer fifty years of opprobrium and captivity so that

their descendants may be happy in the year 3000. Some university professors have become completely possessed by the Demon.

Other less disingenuous disintegrations abound, such as some that the frequenters of nocturnal cafés defend with more loquacity than labor. They talk about art, and are the only ones who can create it: they belong to the first generation that has treated "painting" as "painting," "music" as "music," and "literature" as "literature." While revising the history of the arts, perhaps they discover—and as a result are greatly scandalized—that the robust Titian loved beautiful women to excess, Raphael gave too much importance to geometry, and Rubens was a slave to mythological themes and to a splendid counterpoint of female bodies and the laces and silks in which they throbbed. They, the new artists, will give Paris the new, dizzying spectacle of art completely freed and disintegrated. The atomic revolution is being carried out in the arts too, and critics seek the strangest and most confused words to define the phenomenon. People repeat formulas that they do not understand, just as the adepts of hermeticism used to repeat "abracadabra." In order to sell his merchandise, the new painter of genius has a beautiful beard, anticipates the vocabulary and pedantry of his commentators, and—like a modern hermit

shouldering all the sorrows of civilization—goes for
weeks without taking a bath or visiting a barber.
"And with what materials I work!" he says to us
proudly. "I have produced a revolution in technique.
All painting and all the esthetic concepts that have
prevailed until now have been rendered extinct," he
tells us ostentatiously.

But after having heard these things, these words
that flow on the dirty river of our epoch's commonplaces, I resolved to shut off all diabolic relations.
The Devil has become antipathetically intelligent.
He talks like a contributor to the *Nouvelle Revue
Française*. I shall go back to look at him, perhaps
to admire him, in the vital, disguised, immeasurable
representations carved by the Gothic sculptors. The
excessively "devilized" Devil, like painting that is
only painting or literature that seems to be only
autonomous words, has lost for me a little of the
flavorful, piquant condiment of life.

A Treatise on Novelería[1]

❦ · THE SAVING TRUTH AND DEVOTION

TO THE NOVEL

The Spaniard, who, so surprisingly having conquered the world, became used to deprecating it and created, as no other European has, a literature of "naked truth," never cheerfully loved fashion or changing novelty. He evolved words to express fear and deprecation of what was too "new." One of those words is *novelería,* with its corresponding epithet, *novelero.* And according to the Real Academia

[1] Translator's note. *Novelería* may be translated as excessive devotion to the novel (in both English senses of that word) and novelties. *Novelero,* the adjective, means friendly toward novelties, novels, and tales, and has the secondary sense of fickle or inconstant; it is also used as an adjectival noun.

Española, which sometimes stammers and is ashamed to define, *novelería* is love for and inclination toward novelties; he is *novelero* or a *novelero* who cultivates and disseminates them. But, Spanishly speaking, that affection for "novelties" does not seem as honorable as an affection for bullfighting or *cante jondo*, and *"novelero"* traditionally is used pejoratively. Up to now, the idea of "progress," which implies continual novelty and coincidental changes, has not incorporated profound reality for the Spaniard in the same way as, in adaptation, it has for Anglo-Saxon pragmatism, with its extraordinary culmination in the United States, and—less strongly —for the rational logic of the French. While Europe since the Renaissance has projected the fortune of the world toward the future in permanent change and improvement, the Spanish soul has preferred to exalt, as in the baroque prose of Padre Nieremberg,[2] the difference between the fragility of the "temporal" and the durability of the "eternal." The idea that "the world does not matter to me" because life is short as contrasted with the eternity of Heaven and Hell may engender two opposed attitudes (and on that point the beatific Padre Nieremberg perhaps did not meditate). On the one hand, it favors the ascetic

[2] Translator's note. Father Juan Eusebio Nieremberg (1590–1641), a Spanish Jesuit, wrote a *Treatise on the Beauty of God.*

who prepares himself for the eternal life and does not wish, for that reason, to be changed by "novelties." But, on the other hand, it also justifies crossroads adventures, the aimless adventures of the *pícaro*. If temporal life avails us nothing, let us face it with mockery, relaxation, and lack of preoccupation —such is the *pícaro's* reply to asceticism. (We should not be surprised that in Spain a mystical and ascetic literature flowered alongside a picaresque literature. The antithesis of the ascetic or of the stoic Christian gentleman as depicted by Quevedo[3] was precisely the *pícaro*.) And Quevedo's prose could pass from the sermonizing tone of his *Vida de Marco Bruto* to satirical, sarcastic action, to the caricaturesque and playful super-reality, built upon the deceptive reality of life, of *El Buscón*. The immediacy of existence was sublimated both ways. In the name of death, all the play of the earthly was devalued.

Perhaps the Spanish rejection of novelty or *novelería* arose from the fact that it adds to the person something artificial and adventitious which is not owing to the originality of the self, but to simple imitation and fashion. The lover of *novelería* ceases to be the same because he clothes himself in the

[3] Translator's note. Francisco Gómez de Quevedo y Villegas (1580–1645) was a notable Spanish intellectual and writer. He wrote light verse, satire, and burlesque, as well as didactic and moralizing works.

forms, habits, and language of others. Spanish adages make no more fun of anything else than they do of someone who substitutes for his authentic self the disguise of the borrowed. *"Aunque la mona se vista de seda, siempre mona se queda,"*[4] one adage says. As against the idealized Utopia of Don Quixote, Sancho Panza exemplifies an almost petrified type of man incapable of escaping from his condition, full of preventions and precautions against the deceptions of the world. Only his love for and fidelity toward his patron, the loyal linking of the squire to his knight, drags poor Sancho through all the dangers of adventure and drives him to try impotently to calm Don Quixote's frenzy. When the fatigues and reverses of the road beat upon his fat and earthly humanity with such force, he will calm himself by thinking that such things are natural parts of service to gentlemen and that one in his lower state need not examine them or analyze them to excess. To what tragic treatment the absurd Don Quixote will subject the very prudent cunning of Sancho! Cervantes's genius takes pleasure in the dialectic of this conversion or confrontation between the almost mineral soul of the squire and the dash toward unexampled justice and honor begun by Don Quixote. Even

---

[4] Translator's note. Literally, "Although a female monkey dress herself in silk, a female monkey she remains."

though the combative impulse to remake and improve the world is what gives the human adventure its greatest significance, at the end of the book Don Quixote, now no longer disguised as a knight errant, is convalescing from his *novelería;* the most valid part of his experience was not the meeting with the phantasmagoric princes, princesses, and Amadises of idealized fiction, but the other life of peasants, innkeepers, galley-slaves, friars, *bachilleres,* and strumpets, the free-floating world that "does not always smell of amber" which had attached itself to his expedition. And an example of tolerance and benevolence which was that spare hidalgo's finest testament.

Novelería and the *novelero* are frequent products of our day because in no other epoch so much as in ours has man suffered the persecution of a prodigal exterior world that fires at him objects, formulas, and words that do not even become fixed in his consciousness. With the most simplified pedagogy, we repeat the "catechisms" and "epitomes" of our epoch even though we do not understand them. What can a "mass man" think for himself when, after a wearying day of labor, he has not a minute for meditating alone or fixing his attention upon a personal project that he may think of as distinct from the projects of others? Less troublesome than the attempt or even merely the explanation itself is to take on what the others are doing and to live as though in a world of conditioned reflexes. How should many millions of men react who find a model available for their business letters and their club conversations and who try to "be up to date" and then are faced with a situation and a struggle for which neither fashion nor contagion by others has prepared them? For the most serious aspects of life (and this was well known to the mystics and ascetics of Spanish literature and to the undeceived prose of Padre Nieremberg) really happen as though in a solitary and non-temporal world in which habits and imitation of what is outside us serve no purpose. Sin and guilt and the gravest decisions that man makes in his worldly struggle are entirely personal and untransferable. And the conflict is rooted in this play between appearance and the tragic reality of the self.

❧ · THE NOVELERO THEME

The theme of fashion or of the acquired idea unrelated to authentic consciousness has been taken advantage of greatly by novelists, and in an enumeration that taxes the memory but little, we can recollect Turgenev and Sinclair Lewis and meditate more fully on Flaubert's *Madame Bovary*, in which to the tragic, sentimental *novelería* of Emma Bovary is opposed the falsely aristocratic *novelería* of Rodolphe and the meek, stupid, erudite *novelería* of Monsieur Homais. All of these books, writers, and characters express a peculiar and perhaps deformed aspect of civilization: the garment of appearances as opposed to the legitimacy of the self. And it happens, in such an almost prophetic book as Turgenev's *Virgin Soil*, that the more primitive the social medium, the greater the catastrophic impact produced by the ideas or hypothesis of borrowed fashion or ideology. As the result of an unanalyzed impetus, the characters in Turgenev's novel set themselves to living by ideas that do not belong to them. They convert into fanatic and rapturous belief what for the faraway creators of those very theories was no more than an explanation or provisional hypothesis of reality. The *novelero* begins by adorning itself in and showing off the foreign and the remote, only then to remain pegged to or fused with the disguise, as the mummy to its shroud. In the view of the great Russian novelist, when we uncritically receive an ideology or mode offered to us—or, according to Ortega's formula, when we elevate to the category of belief what had been an idea—our souls can act with the vicious disorder of "virgin soil"; we endow our stupor and misunderstanding with thankless passion and frenzy. A book that we read and the ideas we adopt from it become for us a sacred and inflexible text, as happened to Don Quixote with the novels of chivalry. And the world of the *novelero,* of what is no more than contagion, imitation, or repetition, embraces as many areas as those which separate the ardent and fanaticized beings of *Virgin Soil* from a character as obtuse and as obedient as George Babbitt is to the habits of the "common man" and the commercial propagandas of the street.

Babbitt presents no other surprise than that of being the *novelero* turned out in a series, like the metal blades with which he shaves each day. He is the necessary caricature of a society as abundant in goods as that of the United States, where a man now has almost no time to choose for himself because choice is being performed for him by the incessant electric and electronic tongues of advertising and business. Millions and millions of like people succeed in dressing and thinking alike in that incessant, pursuing, noisy tumult. They have fallen heir to so many things—machines and purveyors of comfort—that they cannot help looking at life with the most unwrinkled optimism. So as to be a salutary citizen, Mr. Babbitt will read the news in the papers each day and will have no conflicts with state or society—increasingly progressive—because he adopts the ideas of his leaders and the enthusiastic mercantile slogans. He will form a healthy and rosy family free of metaphysical anguishes. Do not an automobile of his own, a clean apartment paid for on the installment plan, the latest models of refrigerator and washing machine, and knowledge of the jokes that John can tell Joe in the certainty of arousing the most jubilant laughter add up to the ideal of a well-constituted family? And when information and more ample judgment are needed about things, the pages of the day's newspaper are brought into his house for that purpose, along with the thick breakfast milk. Perhaps Babbitt looks upon the prosperous universe in which it was his luck to be born as a well-supplied, happy carnival in which there are games and objects for all ages and the trivial music accompanying the little merry-go-round horses invites everyone to march. With slight cruelty, the American novelist describes his character shaving before the mirror, noticing that the soap is agreeably lathery, that his bodily functions are working well, and that his muscles show no slackness. And he seems, in this minute with himself, to wonder if he lacks something, if the days, the weeks that end on Saturday—the familiar day of rest—have not become too monotonous. Or if man's life, our small, insignificant adventure, is compressed with inflexible fatality into a closed chain of habits. Looking down from a New York terrace onto the people going by and doing the same things—buying the ties and hats dictated by fashion and walking along like sheep timed by the clock—perhaps he evokes the savage liberty of another world. But what would Mr. Babbitt be able to do in that hypothetical world of solitude? He does not exist for himself, but for the things that he acquires. He is only the unarmed, perhaps kindly phantasm of a civilization of *novelería* in which the things we buy and those which adorn and clothe us absorb the inner nature of our self. We lose our souls by hypothecating them to things. Mr. Babbitt is the *petit bourgeois* of all parts of the world who fears unforeseen disaster and danger. But has not our civilization been populated in excess by millions of millions of Babbitts? It may be that Sinclair Lewis's character—which it would be unjust to think of as exclusively American, seeing that he populates the entire planet—feels the anguish of his soul, the anxiety of existence, and the compromise to which death calls us, feels them at that morning moment before eating breakfast and leaving for the office when he looks into the mirror and shaves the beard that has grown out during the night. All days turn out the same for the shopkeepers of the calendar, and perhaps he hopes that the new day opening before him

(83

will bring him an unexpected surprise. Is not man—call him Goethe or Mr. Babbitt—the animal that cannot be confused, the one that *expects* surprises? Is not that small charge of dynamite in the surprise what gives gusto and value to life? And among all the varieties of human fauna, some, like Mr. Babbitt's mediocre species, hope that a new instrument of comfort or a new breakfast cereal will appear; others hope for the advent of the radical revolution that they invoke; others a new god or a new superman. But, just as in the familiar topic of *desengaño*[5] so familiar in Spanish literature, death arrives when we have allowed ourselves to begin hoping.

❦ · THE *Novelero* IN *Madame Bovary*

Earlier than Sinclair Lewis, and with more penetrating art, Flaubert traced in *Madame Bovary* the drama and anti-drama of the *novelero* character, of those who believe that a change of things has its correlative in a change of souls and that our desire will produce the miracle. The protagonist of the novel proposes to acquire knowledge of the "sublime" in the daily writings and models of the roman-

[5] Translator's note. *Desengaño,* a word finally untranslatable because of its simultaneous multiplicity of meanings, carries the sense of the discovery of error, of censure, of unadulterated truth, and of warning.

tic fashion magazines and in the false words of her
lovers. Along that path she moves toward tragedy
while a *novelero* of another sort, Monsieur Homais,
repeats like a fifty-year-old semi-erudite parrot the
latest commonplaces of the press and of scientific
vulgarization. He wants to boil down the problem of
existence into maxims and phrases.

When Flaubert was not escaping to a world of faraway fables in which feelings and passions break out
with most spontaneous crudity, he diverted himself
by taking apart and inventorying with impassive art
the repertoire of conventions and myths upon which
social structures rest. Human history and the peculiar adventure called "the novel" are fundamentally
rooted in the conflict between authentic beings and
unauthentic beings; between those who accept their
own law of life and those who swim against a pitiless
existential current. If the poor servant girl of so
beautiful a tale as *Un Cœur simple,* one of the mas-
terworks of the French *nouvelle,* is a being all goodness and ingenuous and moving grandeur, a being
who lives in accord with herself, Flaubert's novels
present another race of characters, people for whom
simulation is the dissimulation of existence, and who
at last confuse themselves with the propositions and
lies that they propagate. That these free loans from
civilization, like *idées reçues,* do us no good unless

(8 5

we know how to subject them to the sorting-out process of consciousness was a problem that preoccupied Flaubert from Madame Bovary to those little
maniacal dwarves of culture imitation called Bouvard and Pécuchet. "What nature does not give [the
University of] Salamanca will not grant" a familiar
Spanish saying asserts; and it could be said that
Flaubert's novels are interested in the destitute history of those who want, but are unable, to integrate
themselves with their desired archetypes. Madame
Bovary was not so pure in her sacrifice as she had
dreamed of being; the wisdom of Monsieur Homais
was not so useful and prudent as he had supposed;
Bouvard and Pécuchet could not live by the best
canons of civilization. Very few people resign themselves to bearing the identity of their own consciousness; most of us clothe life, even though we do not
realize it, in alien garb; we are the mannikins of the
borrowed model. The actors in the theater are
dragged into imitation of the drama they are mim-
ing.

The heroine of Flaubert's drama, the new Iphi-
genia sacrificed to false idols and rites, is the defense-
less and enchanting Emma Bovary. We love her in
spite of her fancy dress. When that country girl
dreams, on her Norman farm under the pear trees,
that life will be beautiful and love as sublime and as

unalterably set alight as romantic novels picture it, she meets—as if to free herself from the mistake of her marriage—the poisonous little group of simulators. And from the time of her first adventure with Rodolphe, in whom she sees her redeemer from the vulgarity enclosing her, her life can only roll along in confusion like the wagon in which, frightened, almost unconscious of guilt, she makes her adulterous trips, or like her aimless wandering on the final night of her abandonment, when she is pursued by the phantasms of her disillusionment. The novelist all but wishes not to be moved—for Emma is one being, one person more among the inhabitants of his novelistic universe—because she expiates the sin of having mistaken the mannikins of her fashion magazines for people of flesh and blood.

The burden of civilization—in the cruel Flaubertian analysis—is that it is full of crippling adjectives. Emma believes that the feelings of the viscount of whom she becomes enamored will have the same splendid quality as his jackets, and that the pictures of graceful women which appear in *La Corbeille* or *La Sylphe des salons* sum up all ideals of beauty. How will she be able to struggle and win in a world of masks and commonplaces? She stakes all her capital on the contents of such beautiful words as "love" and "sacrifice." She converts into substantives and acts the epithets concealing reality; she is unaware of the rules and traps of a cruel social game. She pays with the tears that for her are the sweetest and most ardent prize—oh, that lachrymose mania of Romanticism!—for the deceits and treacheries with which existence punishes her. Or, as the novelist says plastically: "In the depth of her spirit she always was awaiting an event, and like a sailor in danger she cast her desperate eyes over the solitude of life, seeking in the distance some white sail in the horizon hazes. She did not know what that hazard might be, what wind might blow it toward her, or to what shore it must lead her." But the hoped-for white sail would not arrive to save Emma Bovary, the little shipwrecked figure of a little bourgeois drama, for she almost never achieved an accord between the disguise of words and the dialectic of acts, and she had absorbed too much dissimulation. Her shroud was the myths that had deceived her.

In the anti-drama of this story, because personages like him will die old and of explicable natural cause, we encounter—how many times we have encountered!—Monsieur Homais. He is the Babbitt of science and prudence, just as Babbitt would be the Monsieur Homais of security and comfort. He meditates on the obvious when it already seems idle to meditate, and opposes to the torrent of life his false protective rampart of commonplaces. He has been transformed from a man into a succinct and well-thumbed encyclopedia for the inhabitants of Jonville, a village lost in Normandy. He is the *novelero* without criticism or malice, and he believes that he has worked out doctrines so luminous that they clear up all doubt about history, politics, and morality. He has emollients and potions for physical pain in the jars in his shop; for moral problems he also has a repertoire of maxims and snippets of wisdom, and he goes about offering them much as Sancho Panza showers Don Quixote with long string of adages. But those of Monsieur Homais—as Flaubert says—are congruent propositions in accord (or so he believes) with science and with "well-known authors." How happy he feels over living in a century as definitively progressive as the nineteenth and over being a subscriber, even at times a spontaneous contributor, to *The Rouen Lantern.* Monsieur Homais considers himself, at the same time, a public servant and hopes that the work that he has written "about cider, its manufacture and effects" will improve agricultural chemistry in his area, perhaps in all of France. He has organized his head like the little squares of those provincial calendars which contain—along with fixed and movable holidays—maximum and minimum temperatures of each season, civic anniversaries, and "a celebrated phrase for each day." But has Monsieur Homais once asked himself what purpose the celebrated phrases serve? Not even when sleeping with his wife or begetting and playing with his children will he drop his school rhetoric, and he will celebrate all progress and invention. He reduces passion and human chance to a series of abstractions (agriculture, the clergy, agricultural meetings, matrimony, society, the family); when he talks, he seems to be aping the printed word. He condoles with men who lived in "more backward and barbarous centuries," and who therefore could not read the words, oiled with instructive ink, in *The Rouen Lantern*. It is clear to him that humanity must go on marching toward indefinite progress, and he would wish, for example, that "Religions should be in accord with the laws of Physics." Catastrophes and sorrows have happened in all eras, but the advantage of our age is that they are reported in the newspapers.

But Monsieur Homais should have learned how dangerous and deceptive all *novelería* is—if Monsieur Homais had been capable of learning anything outside the pages of his little gazettes—when he advised the pusillanimous Dr. Bovary to operate on the deformed foot of the servant Hippolyte according to the most modern surgical methods as he had read about them in the newspaper. That operation was going to be the most revolutionary and progressive approach of the people of Jonville to the medical sciences of France in the nineteenth century. He was enchanted by the word *estrepopodie,* which differs in its roots from *estrofocatopodie, estrefonpodie,* and *estrefexodopodie*—with which words, which indeed moved the doctor, Monsieur Homais wanted to persuade him to use the bistoury. He will go on repeating his befuddling rhetoric when the poor victim is writhing in convulsions; and he begins both to drive patients away from Charles Bovary, the timid man who believes himself audacious, and to cuckold him. Monsieur Homais's indefatigable *novelería* produces disasters that scarcely dent his shield of words. Flaubert has put him into the novel as a caricature of the commonplaces of civilization and as an ignorant and impassible counselor. How many simple parrots, devoid of passion, emotion, and judgment, are incarnated in him! For him every word is a mask for disguising the tragic reality of life. An authentic being like simple old Rouault, Emma's father, breaks into genuine tears when faced by his dead daughter and says simply: *"Ma fille, mon enfant,"* while the solemn Monsieur Homais overpraises "dignity and philosophy" to the mourners.

In every *novelero*—and this is the gravest consequence of *novelería*—hides a simplifier who would subject the world to his over-certain schemes. In the ingenuous apothecary of Jonville, Flaubert was satirizing the drama of half-culture, of men who take in nothing but news and formulas, as though they were nothing more than suits to adorn and clothe us, but who neither understand them nor adapt them to the fluid changing of reality. And in this anticipatory personage, this boring repeater, is there not prefigured the whole family of "simplifiers" of our time, those men who, later than the provincial liberalism of Monsieur Homais, exercised totalitarian power and authority and wanted to reshape us in the mold of their abstractions with greater force and more inexorable fanaticism than the pharmacist used in his arguments with the parish priest? It would be of the greatest sociological interest to follow the variegated descendants of Monsieur Homais through contemporary history. Flaubert, occupying the free intervals that his novels left him, amused himself by writing into a "dictionary of received ideas" many of the conventions and commonplaces that adhere parasitically to civilizations. The great novelist would have been terrified to know—himself having had the happy fortune to work in an epoch of great intellectual tolerance—that in our day, and under numerous political systems, millions of people are condemned and persecuted with formulas as elementary

as those of Monsieur Homais. There are philosophers, poets, and archbishops, both the religious and
the unbelieving, in innumerable prisons of totalitarianism and intellectual simplification. And the lean
author of *Madame Bovary* would have asked if, with
certain forms and pressures of contemporary society,
certain "slogans" of advertising, business, and politics, we have not set out upon the horrible adventure
of "depersonalizing ourselves" and making ourselves
sillier. Authentically human culture will end when
the great questions about the mystery and anguish of
existence come to be answered by robots.

Time of the Lie

❧ · THE LIE AND CONTEMPORARY HISTORY

Although history has had and has periods lashed
by intolerance, tyranny, and the sort of disputable
truth that fanatics like Torquemada and Robespierre
have tried to impose by fire and sword—and which
frequently also exterminates its propounders—no
other period has been weighed down as much as ours
by lying as a monstrous public business. Never has
lying been on so insane a scale, of so planetary a
dimension, as in the years that began with the First
World War and stretched forward through the century. Launched from the tactical and strategic centers of propaganda, lies were to astonish and confuse

what in 1900 still could be called "innocent peoples."
The lies were not merely those which an old, forgotten writer of the nineteenth century called the "conventional lies" of civilization, but another race of lies
so deleterious that under the Nazis they could convert children into spies upon their parents and in
totalitarian politics could replace the usual ethics of
human relationships with the tactics of the partisan.
That annihilating dominion of the lie, already presented by great seers of the nineteenth century like
Dostoevski, became a poisonous commonplace of our
day. The confessions of the victims who have
suffered from it fill thousands and thousands of pages
of present-day literature. From *The Possessed,* Dostoevski's 1875 novel, to Kafka's *The Trial,* which
could be called a poetic anticipation of the Moscow
trials, there began to be written a history of the contemporary soul as shaken by icy terror and struggling—without yet knowing how to act—in a spiderweb of the most contradictory confusion. The
replacement of faith by science, pompously and boastfully proclaimed by the agnosticism of the nineteenth century, became transmuted into the discord
and demoniac suggestiveness of the ideologies. Men
were no longer preached to, as in the Christian
evangels, with exhortations to abandon home and
family to serve God and help their neighbor, but

were urged to deliver themselves over as puppets to the "Central Committee." And because the "Central Committee," despite its frozen inhumanity, is formed of dehumanized men, what was a lie yesterday can be tomorrow's tactical truth. Or, as Ortega y Gasset says, the reason that each one has is not his, but that which the other has lost. People began to repeat and then to fulfill words, transmuting them into mechanical acts that they lacked the strength and courage to analyze. The Caesarean monsters of the epoch—call them Hitler or Stalin—had been metamorphosed into "Pantocrators," into inflexible, inexorable judgment-passing gods as remote from man, from any palpitating human reality, as the stone-encased god of Byzantine mosaics could have been. In Germany and in Russia, under all the exterminatory regimes, churches were closed in order to impose another universal church of hatred and ecumenical deceit.

Had we been able to resuscitate those philosophers of the Illumination who, in Hitler's very Germany, had dreamed that the expansion of reason would make men more even-tempered, serene, and truthful, they would have been overcome with terror on discovering that, in an era in which books were more plentiful and thought was transmitted more rapidly, men would be pursued and blinded by a larger offensive of lies. Constantly increasing semantic discord, an explosive employment of myths, theories, and words—these were the heaviest weapons of the ideological war that could destroy civilization like unleashed plutonium. That a brother shall not recognize his brother began to be said, as in the apocalyptic prophecy. And like new Saint Augustines, a few men in the fearful period between the two world wars—a Thomas Mann, a Valéry, a Croce, a Bertrand Russell—gathered together the small hope, the fine, clear teaching that by then could not instruct, correct, or illuminate the fanatics. Who bells the mad cats?

In the crushing ideological war, it was not a question of distinguishing, as in every preceding society, between an orthodoxy and a heterodoxy, or of one person's belief perhaps being others' heresy or vice versa. Rather, it was a question of multiplying interpretations of things in the interests of group, party, tactical conventions or accommodations. The partisan had to be ready to receive, without previously examining it, his astonishing nourishment of sophisms, even though it was contrary to the very ideology that had been taught him. Historical objectivity never was more difficult than when a shifting mythical atmosphere was raised around every question, hiding or phantasmagorically deforming it. The most exclusive interpretations of adoration and extermination surged up about facts and personalities known to our generation. What of reason or unreason had the horrible Moscow trials, the fearful search for "traitors" in a tangle of abstract theories wrapped up in heavy Stalinesque prose? How judge on the free, serene plane of universal history such personalities as those of Trotsky or Stalin? What motives lay behind the shameful Munich Pact, from which the Second World War emerged, blind and fully armed? These names and happenings require more exegesis, doubt, and argument than a remote story extracted from a spotted palimpsest. Europe has splendid writers on ancient and medieval history, great experts in Egyptology and classical philology, authorities on the Crusades and on Gothic art, on the life of a fourteenth-century painter, and on the business dealings of a Hanseatic merchant. But how many earn the same respect when narrating only events that we all have witnessed, the documentation for which is not to be found in ruined stones and difficult manuscripts, but in the close consciousness of the people who suffered them? In the very time of proud science and no less self-satisfied technology, a trial like that of Eichmann's crimes goes beyond the cruelty of the Assyrian kings and the Tatar hordes.

Nor is the problem solved by transferring human differences from an ethical context to a purely historical one and speaking of a truth of the right and a truth of the left, as still was possible in the nineteenth century, when the argument for liberty was complemented by another for necessary authority, or vice versa, when the understandable polemic of traditionalists and progressives reigned. That lively contrast between a "right" that propitiates all authority and a "left" that demands all liberty no longer exactly describes an era in which the political phenomenon is penetrated by new technical and social needs, in which the radical contrasts that Marx studied out no longer divide bourgeois and proletarian. A Julien Sorel of our time—even were he as intelligent and audacious as Stendhal's character—would not find society implacably divided between the "red" and the "black," between revolution and the "Bourbons"; and perhaps he would delight in the strange phenomenon of political optics which obliges the red to tinge itself with considerable black, the black to cover itself with some purple. As measured against the 1830 scheme, Julien Sorel would come to realize that the methods and the political philosophy of a Stalin were closer to the "black" of a Charles X than to the republican "red" a romantic revolutionary had dreamed of. In the days that we have lived through, was fascism the "right" and communism the "left," as the most elementary simplification pretended? The

(99

myth of revolution is what turns a political regime sacrosanct; the monstrous Hitler too, in his way, aspired to a radical purification of the world. And the simplifying, exterminatory attitude of the red tsars and black tsars of our days, of ideology transformed into a guillotine, is comparable to that of the person in a well-known French ballade who, in a moment of terror and danger, resolved to devour his children with the honorable and domestic purpose of "saving their father for them." Would not millions of obedient people fanaticized by the hatred and myths of the epoch ask their respective "black" or "red" tsars to swallow them for the familial satisfaction of their "little father"? Having donned in strange mental masochism the appropriate haircloth of myths and lies, many people delivered themselves over as martyrs to be sacrificed to an ideology in which they no longer believed. At the Moscow trials there were surely not only innocent victims; there were also sincere confessions of imaginary guilt. In the psychological confusion of the epoch, the official lie could move on to "brainwashing." The contemporary totalitarianisms squeeze man, dehydrate his soul in order to produce that extraordinary human (or already infra-human) *"Ersatz"* called the "party member." We know of many people who had talent and lost it when some mediocre inquisitor forced them to think and write in accord with daily watchwords. More than forty years of tyranny had to pass by in Russia before some recent films and novels could return to describing love and the most spontaneous human emotions, and even then only with modesty as shamefaced as that of the most conventional young Victorian English girls.

And in the terrible "concentrationary" times, which we now hope lie behind the civilization through which we have lived, official untruth was accepted by and affected the most judicious of men. An average college student would have rebelled against the absurdities of a work like *Mein Kampf,* that barbarous Koran of Nazism. But tens of millions of Germans received it as the obligatory wedding gift: on the bridal bed it was to replace Heine's *Buch der Lieder.* That these tactical lies may still be driving human consciousness backwards and have led us into a moral labyrinth, perhaps one without exit, is one of the problems of our time. So-called Occidental culture will be transmuted into the solitary luxury of men who think, write, compose music, or paint if before going forward we do not wash the face of the history through which we are living, cleansing it of large splotches of deception. Let us discover why and for what the lies are told and then denounce the universal liar.

❧ · ON THE WALLS OF PARIS

Let us analyze those forms of lying from a city like Paris, which has the reputation of being the most cultivated, the most non-conformist city of the world, and for that reason is supposed to be most resistant to the confusing aggression of badly used words. Paris has been the most millennial capital of logic and good syntax. But it would be a false picture of culture to suppose that in highly civilized Europe all Frenchmen reason like Descartes or that all Britons proceed with the caution and analysis of a Locke. Our epoch knows more causes of collective deception than were known to the bewigged, ceremonious time in which the English philosopher wrote his *Essay concerning Human Understanding*. Around the ideologies that politicans forge and which sometimes are the accelerated by-product of philosophy, semantic discord often breaks out. A new dictionary of universal concepts would be required, for example, by an unprejudiced passenger passing from West Berlin to Soviet Berlin between one subterranean station and another. In one zone it can be said that the Russian troops entered the city when the Third Reich crumbled apocalyptically, whereas the red banners of East Berlin celebrate the festival of the "liberation." If American troops had been established there, the talk would naturally be of "imperialism." And as a result of being so mistreated, verbal formulas surely come at last to create a stereotyped certainty, so that perhaps young people who have grown up in East Berlin since 1945 believe that the Soviet army truly liberated them. The flexible and agile human condition, which is capable of heroism, also can become accustomed to lies. And just as, according to the critique of Jaurès, the bourgeois democracy of the socialists at the beginning of the twentieth century sent men to stupid and ferocious colonial wars in the names of "patriotism," "national prestige," "the civilizing mission of the white man," and other analogous myths, so the truth was not established when the communist countries exchanged Rousseau's doctrines for those of Karl Marx and aggravated the result when the "monolithic firmness of the State and the Party" liquidated the opposition. The contemporary soul stutters in a conceptual Babel. How pure and candid the Christian evangel when it wanted to disseminate words of good will over the face of the earth so that they would be understood by all! Now the archetype of universal morality is exchanged every day for the ethical relativism of the party member, and Cain is allowed to eliminate Abel when he does so in the "interests of the party" or for the hypothetical triumph of the "revolution." Even in a city as tolerant, refined, and cultured as Paris, words and manners of defining the world change as one goes from one neighborhood to another and reads what anonymous fanatics have written on walls.

Each day of one spring it pleased me to leave my house early, to buy contradictory newspapers, and to look at and reflect upon the inscriptions left on the walls by those political militants who carry on a sort of unsleeping, anonymous journalism. From the clandestine clubs fan out in secret organization the watchwords that will awaken the Parisians along with their milk and breakfast *croissant*. More hatred than love is expressed in these urban graffiti, for although some fervent adolescent wrote a "*Vive Brigitte Bardot!*" the predominating words are "*Morte à . . .*" and "*A bas . . .*" There emerge for the sociologist the words for that wished-for and necessary "modern dictionary" of lying which should complement the modern *Larousse*. Because President de Gaulle said that the destiny of Algeria—at a moment when all colonialism was dying—should be decided by "self-determination of the Algerians," which was only the very honest application of the very French, democratic, and universal theory of the sovereignty of the people, the rabid "*ultras*" who defaced the neighborhood walls compared him to M. Thorez, the well-known long-time chief of the Communist Party. They wrote, for example, "De Gaulle is just like Thorez" or "The cross of Lorraine [the familiar symbol used by the General during the French resistance] is the same as the hammer and sickle." Liberate the patriots—*"Librez les patriotes"*—signified to that same infuriated extreme right that no trials or just imprisonment should be visited upon men who rebelled against the legitimate government and left *"plastics"* in buildings and public places.

My neighborhood (against my tastes as a simple citizen) was showily bourgeois and seemed to have been selected preferentially by the activist *"ultras"* for their war of walls. But if I went to one of those poor streets, picturesque and noisy, in which the Algerians usually lived, the words and slogans changed meaning. The "patriots" (a word so much repeated by right and left) no longer would be Frenchmen in rebellion against the government, but Arab groups who practiced a different species of terrorism. Who, then, are the patriots, it seemed fitting to ask with the greatest semantic scruple upon moving from one zone of Paris to another. And if I had prolonged my stroll, surely another wall would have told me that the true patriot was M. Thorez, who, in then recent days, had expelled some of his old-time confreres from the Communist Party in the name of truth.

The Frenchman is too cultivated (perhaps even M. Thorez, when bored by the "monolithic" prose of his party, used to read Montaigne, Voltaire, Renan, and Anatole France, masters of tolerance and human skepticism), and I do not believe that he ever gave excessive importance to the daily supply of lies harvested from the walls. Furthermore, France has other sources of information than hidden journalists who fail to sign their names. A country sensitive as few countries are to moral analysis, France happily does not lack writers who discover the thread of justice in the daily weaving of propaganda and deceits and still are able to speak to us in the name of a universal ethic that transcends parties and ideologies. But what will happen in places where sclerotic watchwords meet no resistance, where public opinion, with no right to dissent and no heterodoxy, is imposed by the ruling power? That the prophesied revolution about which the humanitarian socialists of the nineteenth century dreamed produced, not intellectual liberty but, on the contrary, a more limited and foolish world—that is the horrible paradox of our epoch. The sterility and tedium of literature and art like those of the Soviet Union are those of the lie and the regimented convention, of the commissar prosecuting the creator, and of the official topic— which all understand and by which all are bored—

deified as "Socialist Realism." What would the great Russian writers—those who fought with all the demons of the human soul, like Dostoevski; those who, like Chekhov, expressed with profound internality the melancholy contradiction of all existence—what would they make of the books that the factories of the Soviet State have set themselves to producing like rye bread and steel ingots? Can we know if the hope of man under the totalitarian Utopia is a world of tedium, of impressive government and technology, but of beings for whom life will be like that of the ant hill—a sum of conditioned reflexes or a docile, blind obedience to slogans? What would Gorki in his paralytic's chair have thought if, after his polemics with Lenin, he could have seen Russian literature also paralyzed by rules, suspicions, and bureaucratic prosecution? For all human creation—as was taught by Hegel, Marx's master—arises from struggle and antithesis, and man's basic truth resists being repressed and regimented. Like every other weapon of domination, the lie is also a weapon of death.

❦ · THE TACTICAL LIE

Before being expelled from the Communist Party, the Italian writer Elio Vittorini carried on with his fellow party-members a memorable debate about culture which earned the grim disapproval of the "Stalinist" hierarchs because it had so many nuances. How dangerous writers are, those men of rebellious words, when, brandishing their questions and their doubts, they want to penetrate the Party's steel-clad strategy! It was the moment—as the French sociologist Edgar Morin says in his book *Autocritique*—when the faithful were awaiting the ukases of the red tsar who since 1927 had been interpreting Marxism along the lines of his despotic desire and with equal intrepidity dictating opinions on politics and genetics, on how judges should proceed and poets be inspired. It was the moment of watching for "freezings" and very brief "thaws" from the Soviet regime as a navigator in the Arctic Ocean observes the movement of icebergs and decides to move forward or to furl his sails. Stalin was deciding for the consciences of millions of men, was prosecuting their dreams and thoughts and ordering the dogmas that should be proclaimed, using today's words to rectify yesterday's. Never since the Byzantine Empire had people so delivered over their souls and so completely renounced thought to the mood and caprice of a despot. In Western Europe, a few intelligent and militant men of good faith and trained sensibility like Vittorini committed daily hara-kiri of spirit so as to place their conscience in accord with that of Comrade Stalin. But their radical demand for truth could only rebel—as in that polemic—when a few mediocre functionaries made culture and man's spiritual legacy a mere instrument of politics. Vittorini, an eyewitness of Italy's laceration by fascism, had sought liquidation of that deceit in the opposite camp, wanting a new system of conduct. But how many lies were being imposed there!

When he started the polemic, Vittorini had not ceased to be—or hoped to cease being—a communist, and he advanced with timid dialectic (he did not want to be alarming or to desert) over the hot coals of contradiction. But why, he asked, must momentary truth be hypostatized to the point of formulating it in a contradictory principle? Why must we force people to say things that they have not said, why endow them with intentions not theirs? In that resumé of his nausea, he wanted to save his faith from lies, from the mischievous cunning, the judgment *ad hominem* which attributed greatness only to what was communist. He rose up against the automatism and conformism into which slogans had congealed.

Although he understood much, Vittorini did not understand that totalitarian ideologies do not permit doubt, that the lie is their necessary tactical simplification; that by means of it they cancel out, once and for all, all reservations and analysis; that by accepting the official formula without muttering, the party member achieves his "good conscience," liberates himself from temptation and scruple. The solidity of the ideology is guaranteed by doing the contrary of what the Evangel recommends: by seeing all honesty and veracity on the side of the party and by shifting all crimes to the others. Unquestionably one must sacrifice in order to obey—to eliminate the notion of guilt—but are not this order and this obedience the symptoms of the greatest contempt for humanity? Perhaps it is because of despising humanity so desperately and of being certain that they themselves have the unique formula for improving it that the totalitarian regimes disdain the individual man. But is not humanity the sum of all the individual men, of that Peter, John, and Francis about whom the simplest Christian catechism speaks? Thus the tactical lie, a weapon of dominance for the party and the demagogue, produces the destruction of all personal freedom of will. The idea of the free man is opposed by that of the party member and the voter who will serve as the docile instrument of the group. And Vittorini had to convince himself that such a regime of commissars cannot ask for a veracious and disinterested culture. By judging a cultural work in accord with a compulsive political assumption, do we not renounce liberty and spiritual invention, do we not retrogress to the Middle Ages, when authority conditioned everything? Trials such as those at Moscow, in which we punish not only what is done, but also what is thought—or what the judges suppose the victims to have thought—do not seem to be episodes of modern history because they are homologous to the origins of the Inquisition and of the crusade against the Albigensians at the beginning of the thirteenth century. Men like Vittorini and others who, like him, entered communism with a surplus of talent and good faith wanted in vain to free it—by means of the very dialectic of the revolution—from its state of suspended animation, inertia, and continuous police atmosphere. Were not culture and fear incompatible terms?

Out of the "tactical lie," out of truth deformed and the sin of suspicion with which everything that does not serve the interests of the party is covered also comes the destruction of all moral equilibrium. The "tactical lie" was nothing but the deceitful accommodation of facts, their subordination to the constantly more cruel and demanding Moloch of the party, the Stalinesque mood and necessity, and the ration of ideological bran, coarsely ground in Marx's great mill, which the "Central Committee" was tossing to the credulous or administering like a hermetic sacrament. In the great burning of heretics at the Moscow trials, yesterday's heroes and even the first evangelists of the revolution were being transformed into today's traitors. What is truth, who has the truth?—that must have been asked in Russia during the big purge of 1936. It was the great apocalyptic novel that the dying Russian literature no longer was able to write, but which was being written by informers and the police; it was the new, livid version of *The Possessed,* almost the fulfillment of the Dostoevskian prophecy. No other creed ever eliminated its first apostles in so cruel a way. No Byzantine basileus ever wanted, as Comrade Stalin wanted, to be hypostatized into an implacable Pantocrator. And what was going to be the new revolutionary morality was changed into nothing more than the winner's niggardly strategy and opportunism. Well, what would have happened if Trotsky had won the struggle with Stalin and installed himself as supreme commissar? If, in accordance with the Stalinesque concepts, morality is the history that is being made, Joseph Vissarionovich perhaps would have been tried and his name rather than that of Lev Davidovich would have disappeared from the Soviet encyclopedia.

Naturally, the bourgeoisie also uttered and established lies and was in no position to cover itself with a pure-white tunic in the face of communism. Others besides Byzantine basileus and Soviet commissar have reserved to themselves the monopoly of truth or orthodoxy, punishing dissidents and opponents through the secular arm. But above and beyond the social classes and political structures, above and beyond Philip II and Louis XIV, who never wanted it, above and beyond Robespierre and Napoleon, with their exclusive forms of human happiness, Occidental civilization in its confluence of Christianity and humanism has created a system of ethical values that provide means for distinguishing the treacherous from the loyal, the lying from the truth-telling. These norms are based upon man's rationality and upon his unequivocal right to justice, whatever the situation that he suffers. It is not possible—and Vittorini must have thought about this—to make a *tabula rasa* of those theorems of civilization by calling them, with the most ignorant communist catechumens, "bourgeois culture" and by imagining that Stalin thought better than Kant or Spinoza. A writer as intelligent as Vittorini would have to ask himself this question and realize that only by answering it could Marxist socialism be made assimilable to the culture of Europe. What erected so inflamed a frontier between the Occident and the Soviet world was not radical economic justice or the so-called society of workers replacing the old-time bourgeois society, but disdain for the values that had refined civilization, for our timeless image of the truth. Unhappily, a world like that of the Soviet did not have a tradition of free examination and intellectual tolerance like that which, despite the absolute kings, the Occident knew from the sixteenth century on. During the long period of the despotic tsars, which had been prolonged to 1917, no one had worked out "rules for the direction of the spirit." The great literature of Russia, from Gogol to Gorki—unlike that of Western Europe—seemed a literature of wandering individualities, persecuted and marginal. From Dostoevski to Pasternak the best Russian writers have been those excluded from their own country, the "complainers" against their respective "Holy Synods."

What a spirit like that of Elio Vittorini asked of communism was that it give an example of veracity, that it respect, beyond the tactical lie and simplification, the content of a culture that is no longer bourgeois or socialist, but can be called human. Because he fortunately lived in Italy and not in Russia, he scarcely had been repressed and expelled from the party when he again was successfully writing novels. Although he had known so much, Vittorini had not realized that in these times the lie is not only the accepted convention, a useful and egoistic disguising of the truth, the rhetoric with which the interests of the bourgeoisie are adorned, but also something more inflexible and monstrous: a whole system of compulsive faith, a conscious and almost masochistic swallowing of deceit in much the way the saints bore their haircloth. In the mental and moral confusion that the epoch has witnessed, in one of the Moscow trials, had there not been at least one man to die rather than be broken by the lie, just as the martyrs and the blessed had embraced their truth? But in accordance with the livid Dostoevskian prophecy, the names of things had become so confused that at times heroes could not be distinguished from traitors.

Latin America: Proximity
and Frontier

❦ · MYTHS AND FORMS OF UNDERDEVELOPMENT

One of the commonest formulas of our epoch, beloved by the experts who spread international organizations across our planet, is that of dividing us into
developed and underdeveloped countries. This
formula, which usually has some validity in the economic field and is intended to bring about better
division of the goods of the earth and access to technology by backward countries, becomes too sche-
matic when applied to culture and the spiritual life.
For the underdevelopment that defines the situation

116)

in Latin America in terms of statistics—despite the inequalities within the zone itself—is very different from that of other continents, such as Africa, and of many Asian nations. Historically very different territories are those of the African peoples who recently have obtained political independence in which the organization of the new states stumbles against their scarcity of leaders and the rudimentary evolution of their modern culture. Also different are the Asian countries that developed by extra-European patterns and forms until the nineteenth century and those of Latin America, which to a considerable measure today constitute a distant but agitated frontier of Occidental civilization. The style of "factory," with insufficient penetration among the native populations, which chiefly the English, the Belgians, and the French developed in the tropical lands of Asia and Africa, was not the same as the longer process of settlement and racial mixture which the Spanish and Portugese achieved in Latin America. The conquest of America was not a "capitalist" enterprise—capitalism scarcely had reached a beginning in the sixteenth century—but an arrival and adventure of invaders who, overcome by the distance between the Old World and the New, ended up "by founding a perpetual home" (as one of the Indian chronicles says) on the shores and on the Andean heights. And "*mestizaje*,"[1] the cosmic race—of which José Vasconcelos once spoke—was brought about long before the 1810 rebellion occurred and despite the colonial dispute about "the cleanness of blood." What an inheritance of *mestizos* was left alongside the "creole"[2] family (which never was that "clean") all over the continent by the conquistadors from Cortés or Pedro de Alvarado to that Captain Garcilaso de la Vega who became the father of the first great writer of our colonial era. (In an excellent book on the origins of Venezuela, Isaac J. Pardo has demonstrated that the larger part of Venezuelan families is descended from a half dozen Spanish soldiers and settlers of the sixteenth century and from such abundant lineage as that of Sancho Briceño, García de Paredes the bastard, Diego de Losada, Garcigonzáles de Silva, or Simón de Bolívar the elder, who, in the dying years of the century, and like a real precursor of his great descendant, went to the Spanish Court to plead for the rights of those whom he had left behind.)

Thus it was a civilization along Occidental lines, of transplanted Spaniards, which founded during the

[1] Translator's note. *Mestizo* (literally mixed or adulterated) is the word commonly applied in Latin America to a racial hybrid, commonly in part Indian and in part Iberian. *Mestizaje* is the condition of being or the process of evolving such people of mixed racial ancestry.

[2] Translator's note. In most of Latin America, *criollo* is used to describe people born in America of unadulterated Iberian blood.

colonial centuries and in the forms and styles of Occidental life—though the Indians give another color and oddness to ecclesiastical celebrations and to the bustle of the markets—cities such as Mexico and Lima, which were not so very different from Madrid or Seville. The Spanish cathedral, the university, the *audiencia,* and the great central plaza, even the much-feared tribunal of the Inquisition, provided Latin America with very peninsular institutions. Not until late in the eighteenth century did historians as Mexican as Clavijero, Cavo, and Márquez express their sorrow over the destruction of the indigenous world. The keys of communication between the Mayan and Aztec monuments and the Indians and *mestizos* who continued to be born had been broken. In popular fiestas and in folklore, indigenous and Spanish forms became so overlaid that they cannot be separated. The Indians and *mestizos* who had stood out from the humble masses had spoken their complaints and demands in Spanish. A man of the time of the Independence already looked upon the indigenous monuments with that melancholy over something destroyed and not to be recaptured which is expressed in the renowned poem by José María de Heredia.

❦ · THE TEOCALLI OF CHOLULA

The peculiarity of the movement for independence begun in 1810, differentiating it from the indigenous rebellions of the eighteenth century, was that America wanted to communicate with the whole world, trade with England, adapt political institutions that had risen with the French Revolution and the nascent North American democracy; it wanted to be an Occidental world and not the Inca-dom closed to creoles which Túpac Amaru tried to establish or a hermetic Spanish colony closed to the thought and the fecund heresies of Europe, which was the ideal of Ferdinand VII. Thus the great liberators—Bolívar, San Martín, Belgrano, Sucre, and O'Higgins—were men of European formation. And Independence and the setting-up of the new nations between 1810 and 1830 were a new transplantation of Occidental styles.

If Christianity, the Spanish language, and a little European humanism were brought us by the Conquest, the Republic brought the political justice then in fashion, as it had been developed by the English, the French, and the North Americans: "equality before the law," the civil code, the modern differentiation between church and state, and that culture placed at the service of national necessities which

Andrés Bello invoked in his memorable 1843 speech
at the opening of the University of Chile. The Latin
American turbulence of the nineteenth century, prolonged through extended periods of the present century, was nothing but the explicable struggle to ac-
commodate those new forms to a subsoil of archaic
traditions, prejudices, and interests. But did not the
European countries live through comparable turbulence when, beginning in the sixteenth century, they
began to create the modern states? Liberty, juridical
equality, tolerance, and, more recently, social justice
never have been won anywhere without struggle and
convulsion. And despite all the rancorous schemes
that could be erected by hatred or political propagandas, we absorbed our archetypes of culture and
social progress from so-called Occidental civilization.

This does not signify that all Latin Americans
from the Río Grande to Cape Horn became "Euro-
peanized." But the alphabet, technical knowledge,
clothing, work, and nutrition of the indigenous
masses, who have lived almost everywhere as marginal to the creole owners, could not be formulated
in Quéchua, Náhuatl, or Otomí: they simply had
more validity in Spanish. It is much too late to tie
together again the arteries severed by the Conquest.
To return to an autochthonous "Inca-dom"—as Túpac Amaru wanted in the eighteenth century—

would not be to advance but to retrocede into proto-history. Lima became the capital of Peru because in the interplay of interests and cultural and economic relationships that integrate modern civilization it was closer to London, Paris, or New York than the old capital at Tahuantinsuyo. The great writers and artists of America, from the colonial men of letters to Rubén Darío and César Vallejo, sought their models of expression in European culture. We can say that the indigenous sensibility, a form of American melancholy or strangeness, palpitates in the prose of the Inca Garcilaso or in Vallejo's poems, but it comes to us now in the Spanish language, which Andrés Bello described in his grammar as the most necessary sign of our Hispano-American unity.

Rightly, then, to save ourselves from some myths, we Hispano-Americans should remember how much of the deep-rooted Occidental there has been in our historic formation. And without negating an understanding of all cultures, the necessary dialogue between Orient and Occident in which contemporary civilization is engaged, let us examine as of immediate moment the relationships of Latin Americans among themselves and their subsequent relationship with Europe and the United States, the regions most accessible to our knowledge.

❧ · THE LATIN AMERICANS AMONG THEMSELVES

More than one hundred nations now are represented in the international organisms, thirty or forty more than when the United Nations and UNESCO were founded at the beginning of the nervous peace signed in 1945. So that a very Babel of tongues should not reign among the nations, the habit has arisen of grouping them by families of peoples. We are listened to more when, in the great world forums, we speak in the name of Latin America than when we express only an isolated opinion of Chile, Venezuela, or Peru. Confronting the linguistic and spiritual frontiers of Europe and Asia, we form the most closely knit alliance of brother nations. We pardon many abuses by the conquistadors for this marvelous fact, which signifies that from the steppes of the Mexican north to the cold Patagonian solitudes a single *lingua franca* is spoken. And, balancing the convulsions of the whole history, we could say that if Pedro de Alvarado and Pizarro were very cruel, Padre Las Casas brought us the Catechism and the first idea of Christian justice, Inés de Suárez the little seeds of Estremaduran wheat, that Alonso de Ercilla brought us poetry, Vasco de Quiroga the social Utopias, and that Cervantes de Salazar taught the first Mexican *mestizos* of the sixteenth century

(1 2 3

the humanist dialogues of Juan Luis Vives. It is abundant, this common spiritual legacy, the history that we have lived or suffered through together. Not to be disdained is the fact that the civil code that Andrés Bello wrote for the Republic of Chile served as a model for all our countries, nor that in order to consummate South American independence soldiers from Buenos Aires and Caracas, Santiago de Chile and Bogotá, Lima and Quito climbed to the heights of Ayacucho, and there seemed to conquer again the Temple of the Sun. Despite the closed frontiers that dictators and caudillos always try to raise at any moment of emergency, when the false Caesarism of Napoleon III attempted to set up a vassal monarchy in Mexico, or when the ships of an arrogant Spanish attempt at reconquest coasted Peru and Chile, or when the first Roosevelt—Roosevelt the Bad— menaced us with his big stick or Sandino rose up in his thicket, a common Hispano-American conscience stood firm against abuse and injustice. In the hearts of all beat the epopee that Benito Juárez lived, the pistol shot with which José Manuel Balmaceda sealed his life as a populist gentleman, and the heroic transit of José Martí on his white horse, writing by his death the last strophe of his poem.

The avatars of our social and political struggle, that painful search for modernity and justice which has been our history since Independence, engender a well-defined Hispano-American problem. Just as now CEPAL exists—the Economic Commission of Latin America that aims at helping the states over the deficiencies of our development—we are aware that another commission, one of spiritual values, ought to be formed to integrate our dispersed culture. The differences and little nationalisms that still can alienate one Latin American nation from another are no larger than those which, in a united France or Italy, distinguish Brittany from Provence, Milan from Naples or Tuscany. The great chorus of unity can be scored with the familial voices. Few continents bring more races together and go on receiving new immigrants, at the same time integrating them all into a common language. If there are fanatics who look down upon that historic experience and want to foment catastrophes and begin again with a *tabula rasa*, others believe that our progress and change must come from conscious and indivisible American solidarity. No people or group of peoples ever has been liberated by foreign liberators. How much voracity for domination and political oppression commonly is secreted in the disguises of the ideologies! The wolf who ate Red Riding Hood can clothe itself in the innocent disguise of a good proletarian. And even through all the oscillations of an impudent

history, the Latin Americans by now have absorbed
too much liberalism to allow tardy application to us
of a regime of Chinese ant hills. In the confused
paradox of contemporary life, many who wish to call
themselves progressives are that only in asking that
their chains be riveted on again.

❦ · THE CONTINENTAL AMERICANS

Because of living in America and sharing seas
and frontiers with the other Americans who founded
the United States and have carried on a more prosperous material enterprise, we must establish clearly
our relationship as neighbors. Otherwise they and
we—as the saying goes—will remember Saint Barbara only when it thunders. The "splendid isolation"
in which the North Americans wanted to live com-
fortably, like potentates in their mansions, ended for
them decisively in 1939, when Herr Hitler and his
Nazis tried to swallow the world. From that moment
on it was necessary for them to establish and negoti-
ate friendships. In the days when Rubén Darío was
writing his ode to the first Roosevelt and United
States marines were debarking in Santo Domingo,
Panamá, and Nicaragua, and Theodore the hunter
was menacing us with his big stick, we could not
hide our outrage and resentment. But perhaps the

consciousness of both Americas now has matured sufficiently so that the poor neighbor does not resign himself to serving his rich neighbor at a sacrifice, but proposes to convert himself into an industrial partner. An hour of justice and equality has arrived for the common destiny of America. The march of the world and the wind of change that is blowing everywhere oblige formulation of those relationships in a manner very different from the way they were conceived in 1905 or 1920. Neither do we wish to go on being intoxicated with sterile rancor, nor they to continue vainly their unilateral predominance. Nor can Chile or Venezuela now be told to hold back its industrialization until the State of Texas catches up. At the time of Rubén Darío, a ship sailed once a week or once a fortnight from New York to the ports of the Caribbean. It could leave occupying marines or interventors in more than one Central American customs house and then return to the United States with its docile cargo of bananas and coffee. In our days of the jet plane, Santiago de Chile is closer to New York than New York was to Chicago by train in 1910. In contrast to the predominatingly rural Latin American societies of the early part of this century, an urban world of almost monstrous proportions now has grown up there. In this thoroughly intercommunicating world, even illiterates begin to understand for what and for whom they are voting. The vestiges of archaic, privileged, or feudal society which hang on in Latin America are beginning to recede before the advance of new structures. And the Latin American multitude aches to create industry and technological advance as the United States created them at the end of the nineteenth century. Despite the so-called "Latin character" and the vocation for the siesta falsely attributed to us—the siesta, in any case, never was enjoyed by more than a few—in some of our cities people have commenced to live with the economic frenzy and the urge toward technical exactness familiar in the North American Babylons. And the only dilemma—as President Kennedy seems to have understood—is that of choosing between the now impossible forms of a hostile economic colonialism and another style of active cooperation which, by improving social conditions, saves the blood that could be spilled in the blindest of revolutions.

From this point of view, the Alliance for Progress could be turned into the most significant American fact since the days when we proclaimed our political independence. We are going to fraternize in the language of techniques, which today are attempting to conquer human inequalities. We have a common project, that of filling the immense empty areas with production and active people and of combatting ignorance and misery, the sad companions of economic backwardness. Other visions of accord exist in Europe, which has created the Common Market and not only has recovered from the disasters of the Second World War but also is more prosperous now than before and offers us an example of miraculous transformation.

Because in recent years all sorts of propaganda have been launched against the United States, because Mr. John Foster Dulles sometimes represented nothing more than a torpid proximity, because avid financiers fenced in and overpowered men of spirit, and because a curtain of tyrannies and vernacular fascism was frustrating the Latin American world under Perón, Trujillo, and Pérez Jiménez, we could do nothing toward a true and authentic understanding. We could say that on our continent the struggles upon which Anglo-Saxons and Latins entered in the sixteenth century, in the epoch of Philip II and Queen Isabella, were being prolonged. If some North Americans resembled the first colonials of Walter Raleigh or of Francis Drake, some Hispano-Americans wanted to avenge Philip II. But all real politics consists in sublimating passion and converting prejudice into service. There was a time—in a year as remote as 1806—when Jefferson and Francisco de Miranda set out to discuss what America could make of itself and what it was called upon to offer toward the concord and conciliation of the world. Those also were the years when, from Mexico to Chile, the Declaration of Independence served as a model to our peoples for raising against metropolitan Spain their demand for political independence and a democratic society. In that way, the American understanding of America, imposed by geographic and economic contiguity, will be the task of good Americans. And, rising above the myths of xenophobia and nationalistic deformation, it is necessary to say that not all the "bad Americans," the "villains" of an incomplete fable, came from north of the Río Grande. As detestable as Mr. Danger or the "Papa Verdes" invented by Latin American fiction were the southern dictators who were put at their service, and an equation was established between the abuses of imperialism and those of our domestic tyrannies.

A spirit as just and as fervent as that of José Martí, who knew the United States for all that was good and bad in it, urged then, at the end of the nineteenth century, that an equitable balance of our relationships be drawn up. He denounced the greedy aggressor, but also knew how to reveal to us the other United States of Emerson, Lincoln, and Whitman. He who was the last Latin American liberator had not stopped learning the lesson of democratic advance, of creative effort, of education for all, which the United States of those days already offered as against our terrible lack of equality. And because, in the long tale, we wanted only to point out the offenses, it is worth taking the time to know precisely the positive factors that can help us toward living together. It was an honor for the world that, when the Europe of the Second World War seemed the booty of two or three totalitarian Caesars, Franklin Delano Roosevelt should have been speaking and fighting for America. Also, within the continent, a juridical system of inter-American relations has been prevailing despite everything, as against the politics of "manifest destiny" and the "big stick." To make this living together more practical, fertile, and equitable is the challenge that we face.

It would be stupid if, in order to shut ourselves up in a regressive autochthony of feathers and arrows or to continue the colonial struggle of the Holy Inquisition with piratical heretics, we should refuse to absorb the scientific, social, and technological experience that the United States offers us. We are not going to renounce our own soul by learning it and taking advantage of it, but we shall be amplifying our universal comprehension. Friendship—when friends respect one another—is the antidote against arrogance and envy, two mortal sins that at times have poisoned our American relationships. Defend us from that savage autochthony which would not improve the libraries, the industrial equipment, or the laboratories if to do so means using methods that have proved their efficacy in the United States. Such petty nationalism already had been answered by the great Latin Americans for whom Independence did not consist of returning to pre-Columbian America, but in our also carrying out all the enterprises and responsibilities of modern civilization. That was the prospect of a culture conscious of its historic position and intending to explore the future, as in Andrés Bello's instructive speech of 1843. The teaching and program of that great humanist almost coincided with similar words spoken by Emerson in Boston when he charted a generous spiritual course for the then very young United States.

In the clamor of propaganda and ideologies which poisons our epoch, any cultural and political problem such as that of a balanced relationship between the two Americas requires a therapeutics of objectivity. We may resolve the problem, not by pronouncing disheveled harangues of distrust and jealousy, but by working toward the new fact, the consciousness of justice which paves the way for legitimate co-operation. A friendship based on squared accounts is necessary rather than any inflamed reticence. In the great American house, we Latin Americans now do not wish to be shut up in the third patio—we also wish to enter the salon. Technology, industry, and scientific application to a great social task are not privileges of a single dominant country among little satellite countries. The six hundred or seven hundred million people who will own the two Americas before our agitated century ends with the year 2000 ask us for a better prospect of the future. If it is not fulfilled from now on, for them and for us—as the popular saying foresees—the Devil can appear before us.

❦ · FRIENDSHIP WITH EUROPE

The relationship with Europe given us by Christianity and humanism, by the rights of man and the political concepts of popular representative democracy, has been expressed in Latin American history in the double and contradictory impulse toward respect for the values of Europe and a certain nostalgia and sense of deficiency because of living on the distant periphery of its culture or because of the disdainful formula of the expert who put upon us the epithet of underdeveloped countries. A young Argentine essayist, Héctor Murena, has applied to the exclusively reverential Europeanism that America inherited a certain parricidal complex according to which the son denies the too powerful, too proud father. Other Americans who have absorbed too much European culture have felt the sadness of the transplanted. To the modernist generation of the end of the last century and the beginning of this one, Europe was an evasion, almost a dazzling and illegitimate pleasure, when contrasted with the solitude and violent combats that characterized our collective existence. "My beloved is from Paris," Rubén Darío said, as though meaning that he must seek outside his narrow Central American home the cosmopolitanism of art and the excitement of culture. From the United States too, at the end of the nineteenth century, and despite the material might of that great country, artists like Henry James went to ask from Europe the serenity and esthetic apprenticeship that their bustling democracy could not give them. Nothing is more indicative in the debate over vocations and intellectual tasks than the correspondence between Henry James, the novelist who left for London, and his brother William, the philospher who remained at home in the United States and offered his people the road of so-called pragmatic philosophy.

Since the time of James and Rubén Darío, both

Americas have increased their historic consciousness, defined their literatures more firmly; the generations that followed them (except for some belated strollers in Saint-Germain-des-Prés) have suffered less from the nostalgic European mirage. We do not picture the great North American novelists of the present century, from the strong, older Dreiser to Faulkner or Hemingway, as so subjected to Europe: rather, they have tried to carry into universal literature the expression of their rapidly changing, dynamic world. The same process, though not supported by a comparable prestige of material wealth and market, can be pointed out in Latin American literature, of which only a few scant fragments have been exported to Europe. But the voyage to Paris and long residence there of a poet as great as César Vallejo outlines his indigenous sorrow with greater pain. Vallejo's "I shall die in Paris in a downpour" seems a desolate response to the earlier hedonistic words of Darío. The happy world of the modernist tapestry, of the "room in the *café galant* where she met her new lover, a pallid pilgrim from a distant land," begins to be filled with astonishment when the way leads down from the frivolous *"belle époque"* into a world of anguish and shadows. Darío himself had noted the transition, and his spirit of a big juvenile faun became more meditative and perplexed when he passed

(135

from the verbal fiesta of *Prosas profanas* to the poems of his maturity, from the ornamental swans of his first song to "the flight of crows" with which he warned of the European war of 1914. The world that came into being then was very different from the carefree modernism of 1895. I do not think that the styles of Paris or London can be imported in very large quantity by any American writer of today—and, in any case, those styles themselves reach the cities of our continent too quickly. Although we may need to go on absorbing the culture and the worked-out methods of Europe, our peculiar situation demands its own authentic and definite expression.

From reverence and docile apprenticeship, we want, in our European relationships, to pass to another level of increasing responsibility within a civilizing destiny. It is time to say that at some tense moments of contemporary history we look with terror at that eclipse of the Christian ethic and of the rights of man which, with the barbarous Nazi regression, threatened all of Occidental culture. That was the instant at which that other Europe of the transplanted which also is called America had to speak out for the cause of menaced man in the words of President Roosevelt. In the Second World War, Europe had to expiate the shameful Munich Pact, the opprobrium of the concentration camps, of the Warsaw ghetto, and the killings of the "non-Aryans" ordered by Hitler. Merely to save itself, European civilization began to understand that one of its necessary frontiers is in the American world. The disciples of Europe had to remind their wise mistress of some ethical and juridical norms that she was forgetting. Now, in the midst of the recurring cold war, we are propping up the complex peace of the world by means of always shaky international organizations. What an ecumenical colloquy present-day universal history offers, what a borrowing of ideas and aid to save us from the major catastrophe and transform Babel into concord, into an authentic human civilization!

It is not only by the formulas of technical assistance, with which in today's world the best-developed nations must assist the deficient ones, that we establish our co-operation with the Europe that has succeeded in rising up with greater transforming opulence from the test of the last war. From the new Germany to the new Italy, the European continent again is seeded with factories, laboratories, scientific and technological institutions. It found the way to transform yesterday's fear into hope. It is showing impatient peoples that work and education are the best revolutionary weapons for improving social conditions. Had Marx been born in today's Europe,

(**137**

his prophecy would have been different from that of 1848. New techniques for conjuring away the fateful are beginning to be studied. For peoples who study and work, the revolution does not now operate on the barricades of the infuriated and the violent, but in the investigations of the scholar, the economist, and the sociologist. What smooths out the disparities of underdevelopment is not the shouts of the demagogue and the cross-country adventure of the *blouson noir* while rebelling and embracing a new terrorist faith, but the will to justice and inventiveness. To save the blood that was the combustible of the old revolutions, to free ourselves from the fear and misery that still weigh on many peoples—that is the challenge to which we are invited by this proud civilization, which from the narrow earth now dashes off to explore the stars. But what should we go out to seek in interplanetary rockets when we still have not achieved concord and equity in our terrestrial home?

In Latin America we suffer—as though from an impatient infirmity of adolescence—from the romanticism of autonomous subversion. But when the intractable and choleric men who now make so much noise in large or small outcries have discharged their violence, they will find out that they must study seriously many things that they do not know, as otherwise—if the Occident disappoints them—they will

have to seek in faraway China the terrible surgeons
of compulsory order. There are false revolutions that
end up deifying the political police or turning over to
them the heads of their own creators. Or does historical experience teach nothing and was not the
fever of violence from which highly cultured Europe
suffered in the third and fourth decades of the
present century liquidated in the bombs that fell on
Berlin, in the Nuremberg trials, or in the phials of
poison drunk by the Nazi hierarchs?

If underdevelopment, which many Latin American countries suffer from unequally, can be conquered only by means of all the material and technical resources of today's civilization, it also requires
that humanism and that Christian ethic which, in the
midst of the very uproar of the Conquest, a Bar-
tolomé de las Casas and a Vasco de Quiroga wanted
to sow in the New World. In a Spanish poet's image,
the discovery of America seemed to widen the meaning of the pilgrimage of medieval faith which ended
at the *"campus stella"* of Atlantic Galicia: another
Milky Way began out beyond the *"finis terrae"*[3]
where Europe ended and hope glowed in new con-
stellations. America rose up out of the grandiose

[3] Translator's note. *"Campus stellae"* directly and "Milky Way"
(*camino de Santiago* in Spanish) indirectly refer to the shrine at
Santiago de Compostela. *"Finis terrae"* is, of course, Finisterre—
and both mean Land's End.

adventure of circling the earth and bringing the divided family of men together in new peoplings and pilgrimages of argonauts. Whether or not in that new world men would find ways to be happy and to conquer the inequality and war that reigned in the old society was the question that was formulated throughout the sixteenth century by the humanists who commented on that extraordinary adventure, from Peter Martyr to Thomas More to Montaigne. To fulfill the hope that was embodied later in the Declaration of Independence and the thoughts of the liberators still is the best goal of all American culture, that synthesis and concord of the other cultures, of those who peopled and those who arrived, which we ought fraternally to make.

Direction: Point Omega

❦ · A MAN WITH A BAG OF BONES

To seek—in the most remote past folded and crumpled in the geologic strata, in the first human or man-like bones mixed in with the oldest stones—not only the history of life, but also the problem of whether or not it advances in a direction toward a "point Omega" hopefully and perfectibly—that was the great feat of Father Teilhard de Chardin. From the spiritual point of view, his life (1881–1955) and work were among the most fecund and significant that our era has known. His glory and the discussion of him have scarcely begun. The polemics that have swirled around his name still have not been calmed,

(141

but already he is recognized as a Thomas Aquinas of the twentieth century, capable of approaching, in a new and different *Summa,* what since the time of Descartes has seemed broken or split apart in European thought: the data, instruments, laws, and relationships at man's disposition for explaining the world with a feeling of transcendence, of purpose and hope in the human adventure which, in the final accounting, is called Religion. He explained that when a wise man observes and places the data of his investigation in order, he has the superior objective of linking all the facts among themselves, of establishing or re-establishing the unity of life, which is like surprising the secret of God. His mystique and apologetics are only the final reason for his wisdom. His scientific data were so scrupulous that agnostics too accept them. Thus, like Saint Teresa searching for God among "the kettles" of her conventual kitchen, Father Teilhard believed that He could also be encountered in the laboratories of a school of sciences and even among the best society of so-called heretics. What fervor and universal tolerance his thinking displays!

The evolutionism that Father Teilhard accepted and completed, the strange line that led from the primates and the remotest age of the proto-humans to *Homo sapiens,* gave him his example of progressive cosmic consciousness. Even in Holy Scripture it was said that the world was not made in a single day, and the final day, that of man and consciousness, came after millions of years. But perhaps—and this is Father Teilhard's novelty—man's day barely is dawning on the horizon of history. Despite the catastrophes and collisions that the process entails, we can have faith in what man, that recent arrival in the immense world of life, still is capable of doing. For the kingdom of the spirit—this is his hope—we are in an early moment of creation. Nor is there between our matter and our spirit that frontier which all dualistic philosophies insist upon pointing out. They are properties of a single thing, unifying forms of a totalization. Biology is submerged in the most variable river of history. In a Bergsonian way, we could say that the dimension of time exists in the consciousness of the man who measures it.

Born, like Pascal, in the Auvergne, that old volcanic area of France which preserves the fissures and crevices of a millenary plutonism, Father Teilhard seems to resemble Pascal not only in his perceptive capacity, but also in his interior fire, the awakeness of his spirit. And at times, when not writing about paleontology or prehistory, he shares the vicissitudes and sorrows of man in an almost Pascalian prose. Pascal was not only a great writer, but also one of the creators of the physics and mathematics of the modern age, and Father Teilhard has

(143

been, since Darwin—whom he completes and ampli-
fies—one of the men who have defined what, in the
language of his books, he calls the "human phenomenon," the primordial chapter of all biology. And
how Pascalian, at the same time, was his combat
with the too literal and too rigid orthodoxy of some
of his superiors, who feared that his science and the
free ardor of his work would precipitate him onto a
dangerous heretical road. Most painful in accent is
the letter that, already in old age, he wrote in 1951
from South Africa to the President Superior of the
Jesuits to defend his Christian faith against intrigue
and calumny. He wanted all to understand that if he
studied the sciences with the most serious objectivity, that was because his spiritual life always was
dominated by the "feeling of the organic reality of
the world" and because he was attempting to discover the sense of a "general convergence of the
Universe." Christ, the word of God, the word of redemption and of hope, lay for him at the end of the
long evolution of our species. They were the "point
Omega" of the exploit of life's conquest of consciousness. In his final theology, the "spirit of God is not
separated from the spirit of the earth." In his view,
given the testimony of the man of science, that unity
could be perceived in "the newly discovered and
formidable dimensions of experimental reality."

Why must it be heterodox to believe that the world has been in process of creation throughout a long series of biological stages, that the higher forms proceed from the rudimentary ones, and that man—that belated inhabitant—has an influence on the incomplete process of perfection and change? In the theology and, I should say, the biology of Father Chardin, neither God nor life nor consciousness rests after having "made," content with the forms achieved; and from the bones and the coarse scraper left behind by paleolithic man to the poetry of Shakespeare and the most complex structures of modern technique, movement forward is in a progressive direction: other steps in the series are climbed. For this new theology—if thus it may be called—the sky is not so separated from the earth, nor transcendence from immanence, and man is a collaborator of God. He is given the earth and he must put it in order and govern it. We still do not know how many secrets and forces are to be extracted from life and matter. Perhaps man has not learned to recognize all that the world contains or how much he will release from within himself. Adam did not make an inventory of the Garden of Eden. The history of our past is only the prologue to and signal of a cosmic destiny.

Father Teilhard was searching for it with his

geologist's hammer, his classifying hands, during a scholar's exhausting periplus in the least-known regions of our planet. The Sorbonne had taught him science and tolerance; the First World War, in which he was a soldier and stretcher-bearer on the fields of Verdun, enlarged his human experience in sensibility. The Moroccans with whom he lived in the Fourth Regiment of Zouaves and Fusiliers, and whose wounded bodies he tended on the convoy stretchers, called him *sidi marabout,* which in their language is an affectionate term for comrade and friend. There too he learned the serene courage with which, on his two great Asian expeditions through Mongolia, Turkestan, the Gobi Desert, and Siberia, he resisted hunger, thirst, and loneliness. During those years of great revolutionary agitation in the Orient, the little caravan suffered from assaults by bandits and guerrillas. They were times of political torment in Central Asia, struggles of provinces against provinces, leaders against leaders, Communists against anti-Communists, Japanese against Chinese, and Father Teilhard, who was one of the world authorities on prehistory, who had discovered the footprints of the first sinanthropes in the loess beds and folded strata of the desert, meditated on the other changes and disturbances of the historic being. What a shame, he once said, that men during their short life, so short in contrast to the millions of years that preceded their appearance, have not yet learned to stand side by side rather than against humanity, as in the waste and horror of all war.

For the time being—in those days from 1923 to 1936 in which he carried out his major Asian expeditions—Father Teilhard was no more than a tenacious and absorbed investigator carrying across the steppes and Chinese valleys his bags of fossil bones and reconstructing the work of those first, already industrious, proto-men who must have lived on the lands that emerged from the last Tertiary period. What relationship they bore to the other proto-human *Pithecanthropi* of Java and India was what he wanted to read in the strata. But as, besides being a paleontologist, he was a mystic and a thinker, his almost desperate purpose was to discover in the long evolution of the species the subtlest evolution of consciousness, and to produce for the people of the twentieth century a difficult *Summa* of man as Saint Thomas wanted to produce the *Summa* of the religious. And whether or not from that past, from the historical process continuing the biological process, he could point out a direction for humanity, whether so much life was not more than an expenditure of material and energy, collections of bones and tombs —that was the question he asked as a philosopher and a moralist. For that reason a sociologist like Gaston Berger, who added to social science in France the new discipline of the "prospective"—that is to say, of a possible acceleration of history through looking in our present position for reasonable data with which to plan the future—saw in Father Teilhard one of the precursors of the studies and projects that could shape the human future. We are going to wring from a colloquy with his books, which are at once precise and fervid, a teaching that can serve us all.

❦ · MAN AND BIOLOGY

Father Teilhard's originality does not reside in his having reconciled his Christian faith with the theory of evolution of species (in his time the past century's polemic between the Church and the evolutionists already was growing calmer), but in his having established with genius what was peculiar to the process. And as against what physicists call entropy—that is, the law of degradation and the tendency to uniformity of energy—what is native to the biological is the complexity of its combinations. By a law of "corpuscle-ization," the elements unite, not in order to merge in homogeneity, but so as to differentiate themselves as more elevated and better-defined individualities. It is unnecessary to prove that today's man has more inventive capacity than the first hominoid *faber* who, in India or Java, on the turbulent geological frontier between the Tertiary and the Quaternary, began to take possession of the Universe. And the law of "corpuscle-ization" gives birth to another, that of "complexity-consciousness," according to which the elements uniting in superior individualities exalt their inwardness, are converted into themselves in centers of action and reaction, perceive, and accede to the reflective. In the beautiful Biblical metaphor, the lump of clay from which man had been formed awoke to the life of the spirit. And what a beautiful myth was shaped in the cosmogonies of all peoples, in that appearance of man, gifted with consciousness and replacing the monstrous animals or—like Prometheus—stealing from Zeus the secret light and fire. On that level, evolution then proceeds by what the Father called "neogenesis." Consciousness gives birth to consciousness, and man as a participant in the creation of the Universe begins to give life direction and destiny.

The geologist Suess had used the word "biosphere" for everything that surrounds what is alive; Father Teilhard called by another new vocable the other, thinking layer, the spiritual heritage that shapes history and is as active and explosive for the

(149

human medium as bacteria can be in what is purely biological. He named "noosphere" that which the spirit adds to nature. It is not a dissociated spirit, but one integrated in the cosmos. With the language of a poet, he imagined that if our planet were to be looked at from outside the earth, it would appear clothed not only in the green and blue of the oceans and the plants and the sores of erosion, but also in the light of thought. The first life, to continue with the simile, was "the purple darkness of matter," but during the immense length of prehistoric times, "the gold of the spirit" also came into existence. Father Teilhard wrote: "I do not know why the geologists pay attention to all the concentric spheres of which the earth is formed except one—that formed by the thinking human layer—whereas those interested in man ordinarily are strangers to geology. It is necessary to combine those two points of view." And in the complex and diversified evolution of consciousness, from the first hominoid *faber* to Shakespeare or Mozart, what the poet calls the "white incandescence of the personality" was being accentuated. "The personal," he wrote, "is the highest stage, for from it we can grasp the fabric of the Universe." The world of the Spirit is a world of "persons." Man imprints the trace of his adventure and his dreams upon cosmic evolution. And upon it is drawn—as we shall see when studying the historic thought of Father Teilhard—the course of a future or, as Gaston Berger would say, the possibility of a "prospective."

In the world of life, the appearance of man was the most extraordinary emergence, and four incomparable properties were concentrated in it: extraordinary power of expansion; extreme rapidity of differentiation; unforeseeable persistence of the capacity for germination and for interrelationship among the stalks making up one sheaf. "A surprising zoological fact, the principal evolutionary effort of the earth was concentrated in man from the end of the Tertiary. In man, life, from the Pliocene on, concentrates (like a tree toward its summit) the best of its remaining sap. During the course of the last two million years, though we can observe a multitude of disappearances, no new reality except man has sprouted in nature. In itself this symptomatic fact should attract our attention and awaken our suspicions." Or, to continue with our Biblical metaphor, man was the last creation, and after it, God rested. Biologically, "humanization" seems a "mutation different from all others in its development."

Man, then, initiates a new dominion or division in the Universe: the sphere of the reflective. Following the line of "humanized" anthropoids, the wave of complexity-consciousness penetrated the earth. "And

(151

once that step has been taken, the process continues being defracted through a complicated pattern of more or less divergent rays, the diverse zoological radiations of the human group." In accordance with a primary and universal quality of vitalized matter, the "zoological radiations" that are propagated in a psychically convergent medium manifest the tendency to draw together and become linked. Thus is born, in an atmosphere—if not by an effect—of "socialization," the eminently progressive group of *Homo sapiens*. And the human phenomenon brings with it another tendency toward personalization, in the "association in symbiosis, under psychical relations of the histologically free corpuscles," which has been observed in animal colonies. In no sphere of organized life does the isolated individual exist—the savage is born into a group of savages—but the phenomenon of "complexity-consciousness" at the same time increases personalization in man. The "ethnic-social" unifies the whole and integrates what Father Teilhard called the "noosphere," that thinking summit beneath which the peculiar human adventure unrolls. The anthropoid that has turned into *Homo sapiens* differs from every other zoological family in that it is ubiquitous and engenders new paths of evolution by "anthropogenesis," in that it thus not only has a present and a past, but also—as

Father Teilhard wanted to demonstrate—can prepare the future.

It falls to man, as the last arrival in the kingdom of creation, to govern and direct an immense inheritance of life. His youth, as contrasted with the three hundred million years of matter, promises him, according to the prediction of this Jesuit priest, an enterprise that is perhaps only beginning now.

❦ · ANGUISH AND HISTORY

Is it possible to extract from Father Teilhard's thinking a philosophy of history, a dialectic of life that will serve to allay the anguishes, tensions, and unknowns about which present-day man debates, and to combine that double current of "socialization" and "personalization" which, in his language, is native to the "human phenomenon"? Have we been moving from the mists of prehistory toward an always perfectible goal of consciousness? As against the optimism of the philosophy of the Enlightenment and a large part of that of the Renaissance, from the middle of the nineteenth century on, European historical thought began to become charged with perplexity and fear. Tracing parallels between our epoch and other historical epochs, it saw in so-called human progress grave symptoms of decrepitude and

crisis. Swollen industrial civilization could not resolve its own contradictions. The wars became
crueler; weapons of destruction and death were
superabundant among man's new inventions. The
prosperity of industry at that time was built on the
exploitation and misery of colonial peoples, on a
ferocious hunt for products and the most miserable
labor in African and Asian lands. Also, while improving technical procedures and the efficacy of machines, European industrialization sank into monotonous labor, badly paid and gloomy for immense
working masses—or, worse than that, condemned
them to unemployment. After the first industrial revolution, the multitudes in the great capitalist cities
seemed—in the name of economic liberalism—more
forsaken, rancorous, and sordid than those of the
Faubourg Saint-Antoine in Paris, who in 1789 had
marched to storm the Bastille. Political rights had
not been integrated with social rights. Alongside the
egoism of the bourgeoisie which Daumier carica-
tured a century ago, the proletarianization of great
urban masses, to whom Marx wanted to give the
destiny of avenging archangels. That "proletarianization" was—not only from the economic point of
view, but also from the spiritual—a serious sickness
of culture. "The rancor of the oppressed was becoming one with the rancor of the masters," Nietzsche
wrote.

And such historians as Burckhardt in 1870 and Spengler in 1920 cited against the old-time propagandists of progress the interior cancer that was beginning to corrode civilization despite its displays of opulence and strength. Humanity was entering upon a period like the one that, in Rome, followed upon the exhausting enterprises of the Empire, in that turbid decadence of forms and of spiritual unity when, after Marcus Aurelius, the Roman world began to die of its own conquests, of the inflation of its arrogance; when on the arches of triumph was incised the melancholy cortege of the day's captives, who would be tomorrow's destroyers; when the serene style of the old classicism was replaced—from the third century on—by the false giantism of imperial art. Burckhardt's book on Constantine the Great and his *Reflections on Universal History,* which followed the Franco-Prussian War of 1870, seem to be giving instance and warning to the new days of implacable capitalism and implacable proletarianization which were emerging on the historical horizon. In Burckhardt's comparative method, no serene solution was to be found in the completely compulsive state socialism or capitalism, destructive of the person, to which Rome came—allowing for the differences and limitations of its technology—at the time of Diocletian. If Christianity arose in order to save the world at that time, in order to create a

"City of God"—then, when a harmonious earthly city was not possible—the devotees of comparison would say that in our age they are offered in Marx's prophecy the promise of a communist "third kingdom." Marx was the anti-Saint Augustine of an epoch that was turning anti-Christian. But in order to achieve the glory of that new kingdom, was it necessary to pass apocalyptically through the Valley of Jehoshaphat of a revolution by which the oppressed could be changed into the new oppressors? What we must save is not only a social class, exterminating the others, establishing equality by diminution—for we also require a more difficult revolution of consciousness in order to establish human concord and equilibrium. Whereas in settling the accounts of contemporary history Marx conceived the idea of the suffering class inexplicably annihilating the one that had made it suffer, Nietzsche invoked the Utopian avenger, not against a class, but against a system of values. With the eternal German romantic nostalgia, Nietzsche conjured up in the image of a new sacrificer of monsters the Superman who would reestablish heroism and beauty. The greatest problem of the epoch seemed to be how to harmonize in society the double impulse to "socialization" and to "personalization," of justice and of creative liberty. In the crass world of the end of the nineteenth century—a world of an abusive bourgeoisie and full markets—a species of salvation through rage already was being invoked, and the anarchists of those days would blow themselves up with their bombs alongside the carriages of princes, grand dukes, and prime ministers. But what still had seemed to be a literary theme in 1890 turned out to be terribly imminent when the European totalitarianisms emerged after the First World War.

In his grand *Summa* of cultures, with the audacity and force of a poet, Oswald Spengler applied the simile of seasonal cycles to the history through which we were living and announced a bleak wintertime. Spengler's moral was that we must bear the oncoming storm with courage, save ourselves through disillusionment now that we could not do it through hope. Like other cultures, ours was about to die of Caesarism, violence, and "massification." We were admiring the great cities in which were crystallized the force, wealth, and profusion of capitalism, but without seeing that the truly creative was disappearing in the solitude of millions of beings, in the uprooted masses lacking unity and a common destiny. As in Rome under the worst Caesars, the demand again was for bread and circuses. Business or the police state, then, was taking over culture, and we scarcely noted its decadence in the "colossalism" or false splendor of the propagandas. Spengler seems to have been writing in 1920 an anticipatory chapter of what would happen in Germany thirteen or fourteen years later. But on the periphery of what still was the dominating European world, other things were going to happen, such as the dark rebellion of the colonial peoples, that great rising tide of the oppressed and neglected against the arrogant which had been the final scene of every historical cycle. After that, the panic and lethargy of spirit would be prolonged for centuries; the death would be long and painful until, in other peoples and other latitudes, the "primary symbol" of another culture would appear and the new barbarian chiefs, born on the provinicial periphery of the ruined empires, would erect over the ruins and empty palaces—as Constantine did—the sign of a new Cross. That we should prepare ourselves for a time of horror—theologically that of the Antichrist—was what some prophets of history were announcing.

The worldwide "situation" between the two great wars of the century, with the diasporas and captivities of whole populations, genocide, and concentration camps, influenced the literatures and philosophies of the epoch. For the first time since humanism and the optimism of the Enlightenment in which the Modern Age was born, man was asking if life has any outcome or direction, if the only factor personalizing us in the face of the world's indifference is our nausea or our anguish, and if in the face of facts we move, like Kafka's characters, through a succession of labyrinths.

Now we shall see how Father Teilhard, who suffered, like all men of his time, from the confusion and bitterness that this century offered—in the trenches at Verdun, in the fearful cortege of the Asian multitudes, blown about by wars and revolutions, in the totalitarian fantacisms of Europe—will seek in a cosmic vision of human destiny the sign of hope which had seemed hidden. The heavy tyrannies that scourge the world, he comments in an admirable letter of October 1936, have forgotten the "progressive energies of the earth" and are ignorant, further, of the synthesis that must be made between "universalism" and "personalism." The "fascisms," he added, "see no hope other than that of taking man back to the days of the neolithic." And in the disorder and contempt of our epoch, we seemed also to have forgotten that for a religious spirit like his love is "the only force that brings about the unification of things without destroying them." Were the totalitarian Caesars of the century revenging themselves on their peoples for their own inability to love? But at that very moment the French sage, who was to a high degree a geologist, a paleontologist, and a biologist, was thinking about a new synthesizing and unifying science to guide evolution and dare to read, prepare, and decipher the future. What will take place and how we shall best prepare the next fifty thousand years is a question that in its audacious and staggering purity deserves to be the preoccupation of a thinker and a philosopher.

❦ · POINT OMEGA

For a profoundly religious spirit like that of Father Teilhard de Chardin, the "point Omega" toward which, by convergence, life leads is nothing other than God. And in Christ—God incarnate, sharer of men's sorrow—he saw a symbol and final destiny of history. But let us not proceed to judge that ultimate mystical frontier of his thought with the smile and incredulous flippancy of some Monsieur Homais, of a personal enemy of the clergy and a rebel against all theology. A man of fine intellectual tolerance, acquainted as few others with the most varied disciplines of modern science, Father Chardin had argued in more than one unforgettable Parisian debate with Marxists, phenomenologists, existentialists; he had meditated not only upon the evolution of the species and upon prehistoric man, but also upon the human task in a time as disordered as the one in which he happened to live. And he was asking that we pay to the mystical element of his philosophy the comprehensive attention that he conceded to his opponents and adversaries. His wisdom wanted to speak to the agnostics too, and outside of the religious sphere he craved to show us how evolution had fulfilled itself and what hope could be deduced from the experience of millennia. If at the end of his life he pronounced the name of Christ with sweet nostalgia and outlined a "beyond science" for which the Christian symbol served him, that was because, according to him, each succeeding epoch will be able to interpret with increasing consciousness the teaching of unifying love which is associated with Christianity. Not by escaping from the world in order to achieve the dissolution of the self—as in the Oriental mysticisms—but by possessing the earth, serving it, and directing it to the advantage of man—that was how his active religious spirit met God. "To build the earth is one of the first human duties." And in his final religious contemplation, the free will and liberty that God leaves to man is given him so that he may finish "building the world." (The Marxists could compare this thought of Father Teilhard's with that of Marx to the effect that man came into the world not only to explain it to itself, but also to transform it.) Yes, that "change of the world" resulted from the progressive evolution of consciousness, from the strength of love, which does not destroy, but reconciles and unifies. In the march of human societies, the two tendencies—that of "socialization" or unification of groups and that of "personalization"—must be integrated. And had not the recent and tragic explosion been that of an anarchic liberalism that split the individual from society and of a compulsive totalitarianism that forgot the person?

Father Teilhard's religiousness—the last step of his meditation upon man—deduced the idea of God from that "sense of the earth" which "reveals to each one that a part of himself exists in others and brings about the appearance of a principle of universal affection in the conscience of the world in progress." God would unify himself in everything, would be reflected in everything, as sunlight is reflected "even in the pieces of a broken mirror." Father Teilhard sets out from the earth itself, and would not—as in the old dualisms—separate body and spirit. Man's exploit in seeking God is not a flight and escape from this world—as in the Oriental mysticisms—nor from the "vale of tears" of the most disillusioned ascetics, but begins with dominion over and acceptance of the terrestrial; from this plot of ground which has been left to man to be cultivated and fecundated so that he may participate in a grandiose work of cosmic evolution. Father Chardin compared it to a voyage, to the new part of it which we must travel each day. It was a metaphor of a wise traveler who had conquered great spaces, had touched and explored many soils (Mongolia, the Gobi Desert, Siberia, Java, South Africa) so as to tie together the eras since the first anthropoids began to move about, then advanced to *Homo faber* and to the already very complex, universalized, and specialized *Homo sapiens.*

But even those who reject Father Teilhard's religious thought can see in his work one of the most fecund and hopeful intellectual adventures of our epoch, another philosophy of history to be set up against that of the apocalyptic thinkers. By an inherent strength of human life—what he called the phenomenon of "complexity-consciousness"—man was not only the tardy fruit of biological evolution, but also a participant in the terrestrial drama as actor and modifier. The collective consciousness completed the "biosphere" with a "noosphere," the spiritual, progressive, and changing ambiance and inheritance that provide the stage of history. In that change of the "noosphere"—infinitely more rapid than biological evolution—Father Chardin's conception of the world is diametrically different from that which Aristotle could have. The appearance of man

(163

in the process of life and history brings about a "neogenesis"; tradition and the human effort in forging social groups, conquering nature, and inventing techniques in turn bring about the "anthropogenesis." In a word, the field of the creative consciousness is expanded. What an enormous distance and what a spiritual horizon separate the first proto-human *faber* from Goethe or Beethoven! Those two forces, of "socialization" and "personalization," in the equilibrium of which the best secret of our anthropological destiny is rooted, struggle and interpenetrate in the historic process. If "socialization" alone had predominated, the human groups would have evolved like colonies of termites or ants; on the other hand, the isolated individual would have sterilized himself in incommunicable confinement. Not only heroes—as Carlyle said—make history, but they do make it too, for the mental ambiance in which man moves seems different when it is fecundated by great visionaries who prepare the future by their acts and thought. All biological and spiritual evolution is irreversible; once launched, the process cannot be stopped. Is it, then, strange that a religious spirit like that of Father Teilhard should inquire whether the convergence toward the future is directed toward a "point Omega," toward an increasingly perfectible teleological goal? It is the image of a God not separated from the world, but immersed in it, moving with it in the abundance of the aeons.

And as artificer and transformer of the world, an actor in the evolution by "anthropogenesis," man is offered the dazzling task of foreseeing what is to come. This vision of the future—which now is asked of history—is another step in the advance of the force of "complexity-consciousness." Too young in the life of the earth, the last arrival in creation, man has a history that scarcely has begun, and the fifty or one hundred thousand years of the first proto-human *faber* and the six thousand of the first monarchies and city-states of Egypt and Chaldea are only one second—a papyrus, a temple, and a sphinx in the desert—in contrast to the millions of years of prehistory, when the planet was almost alone, the continents were emerging, and the monster animals had begun to develop. But in every mythology a Herakles or a Gilgamesh imposes order on the fury of the world, beheads the Hydra and the savage wild beasts, and makes the human "habitat" more serene. "It pleases us to be alive," said Father Teilhard, whose religiousness was established in the brave acceptance of existence and not on the call to death —and that "taste for life" instills a propulsive vigor into the process of evolution. Lacking vital love of that sort, our species would go on being degraded according to the law of entropy applicable to physical phenomena.

"I go toward that which is coming," Father Teilhard had written proudly in some intimate notes a few days before his death. The vision of preparing the future seemed to him, in view of the example of biological evolution and the most complex spiritual evolution, an inescapable problem set before the sciences in our time, the audacious synthesis of what could be an anthropological program. Science would be of no use if it did not assist man in that painful search, if it did not illuminate his way through all the labyrinths. In the most grievous days of the Second World War, lost in China, lacking word about those close to him and of what was happening to his sweet land of France under the Nazi fury, he said these revealing words: "At the root of the greatest disturbance on which the nations have embarked today, I distinguish the signs of a change in the human age. Like it or not, the age of the 'lukewarm pluralisms' finally has passed. Either, then, a single people will succeed in destroying or absorbing the others or else the peoples will join in a common soul in order to become more human. Unless I deceive myself, that is the dilemma set by the present crisis. In the collision of events, may the passion to unite be lighted in us and become more ardent each day as it faces the passion to destroy. Let the peoples who are fighting us recognize that we are resisting them because we can bring them what they have been seeking in vain."

And in 1948, making a synthesis of all the conquests that the theory of evolution had achieved since the days of Darwin, he outlined his historical thought: "A fresh new stage of general evolution is beginning now with man. For not only does man in evolution make evolution conscious of itself (Julian Huxley), but also in man (to the extent to which he socially discovers the scientific procedure for orienting himself toward ultra-reflection) life makes a leap forward under an appreciable and increasing power of self-transformation. If we accept this perspective, a new era visibly is beginning for anthropology. Up to now, this science has been considered largely as a pure and simple description of past and present man, individual and social. In the future, its principal center of interest ought to be that of guiding human evolution, giving impulse to it, and conducting it forward. The neobiologists often forget that underlying the various rules of ethics, economics, and politics there are to be found inscribed on the structure of our Universe certain general and imprescriptible conditions of organic growth. To determine—in the case of man—these basic conditions for biological progress should be the specific aim of the new anthropology: the science of anthropogenesis, the science of the final unfolding of humanity."

Thus Father Teilhard presents not only a "perspective," but also a "prospective" of man that offers —as Gaston Berger has noted—the most hopeful fecundation of historical and social thought in our time. To give constantly greater consciousness to the process of evolution—is that not, like the conquest of space, one of the most promising challenges offered to human effort?

A NOTE ON THE TYPE

THE TEXT of this book is set in *Caledonia*, a typeface designed by W(ILLIAM) A(DDISON) DWIGGINS for the Mergenthaler Linotype Company in 1939. Dwiggins chose to call his new typeface Caledonia, the Roman name for Scotland, because it was inspired by the Scotch types cast about 1833 by Alexander Wilson & Son, Glasgow type founders. However, there is a calligraphic quality about this face that is totally lacking in the Wilson types. Dwiggins referred to an even earlier typeface for this "liveliness of action"—one cut around 1790 by William Martin for the printer William Bulmer. Caledonia has more weight than the Martin letters, and the bottom finishing strokes (serifs) of the letters are cut straight across, without brackets, to make sharp angles with the upright stems, thus giving a "modern face" appearance.

W. A. Dwiggins (1880-1956) was born in Martinsville, Ohio, and studied art in Chicago. In 1904 he moved to Hingham, Massachusetts, where he built a solid reputation as a designer of advertisements and as a calligrapher. He began an association with the Mergenthaler Linotype Company in 1929, and over the next twenty-seven years designed a number of book types for that firm. Of especial interest are the Metro series, Electra, Caledonia, Eldorado, and Falcon. In 1930, Dwiggins first became interested in marionettes, and through the years made many important contributions to the art of puppetry and the design of marionettes.

Composed, printed, and bound by
The Haddon Craftsmen, Inc., Scranton, Pa.